MW01504987

# At the Heart of Matter

Marie-Louise von Franz, Honorary Patron

**Studies in Jungian Psychology
by Jungian Analysts**

Daryl Sharp, General Editor

# AT THE HEART OF MATTER
## Synchronicity
## And Jung's Spiritual Testament

## J. GARY SPARKS

For my father

**Library and Archives Canada Cataloguing in Publication**

Sparks, John Gary, 1948-
At the Heart of Matter: Synchronicity and Jung's
Spiritual Testament / J. Gary Sparks

(Studies in Jungian psychology by Jungian analysts; 119)

Includes bibliographical references and index.
ISBN 978-1-894574-20-4

1. Jung, C.G. (Carl Gustav), 1875-1961.
2. Coincidence. 3. Pauli, Wolfgang, 1900-1958.
4. Franz, Marie-Louise von, 1915-1998. I. Title.

BF175.5.C65S65 2007      150.19'54      C2006-906944-1

Copyright © 2007 by J. Gary Sparks
All rights reserved.

INNER CITY BOOKS
Box 1271, Station Q, Toronto, ON M4T 2P4, Canada
Telephone (416) 927-0355 / Fax (416) 924-1814
Web site: www.innercitybooks.net
E-mail: admin@innercitybooks.net

Honorary Patron: Marie-Louise von Franz.
Publisher and General Editor: Daryl Sharp.
Senior Editor: Victoria Cowan.
Office Manager: Scott Milligen, D.PC.

INNER CITY BOOKS was founded in 1980 to promote the
understanding and practical application of the work of C.G. Jung.

*Cover:* The hole open to eternity—the spiritual pilgrim discovers another world;
19th century woodcut, colored by Noel Taylor, Toronto artist.

Printed and bound in Canada by Thistle Printing Limited

# CONTENTS

*See final pages for descriptions of other titles in this series*

# List of Illustrations

I wanted the proof of a living Spirit and I got it.
Don't ask me at what a price.
—C.G. Jung, letter to Victor White, January 30, 1948.

Two eyes has the soul; the one looks into Time,
The other towards Eternity.
—Angelus Silesius.

Window on eternity; by C.G. Jung.

# Introduction

## A dream of road construction

I give pride of place to dreams, so I would like to begin with one of mine. It will introduce the subject matter of this book, clarify why I am interested in the theme and explain my method in the pages to follow.

I am part of a construction crew and am walking with them through the countryside. We are going to a construction site about half a mile ahead and over a rolling field. I look toward the site and see that the crew that has been working on the project is exhausted. They have done their part of the job and are wrapping up; their work is finished. As my group gets a bit closer, I see that the construction project is a road. The road has been surveyed, leveled, graded, and the first layer of stones has been put down. My crew is to replace those who have just finished and to bring the road's construction to completion.

As we walk along, one of the foremen from the other crew comes up to us and starts talking with me. He explains in some detail the kind of work we will be doing. I listen attentively and then say to him, "Oh, by the way, where does this road go?" He replies, "Between matter and spirit."

This dream inspired me to explore and chronicle the connection between the material world and the spiritual world, or, in more contemporary terms, between the outer physical world and the inner psychological world, as it has been considered in Jung's writings. The dream will guide both the subject matter and the method in what follows. My purpose is to understand how Jung and his immediate successors envisioned the unity between the two dimensions of reality that Western philosophy and science have defined as separate since the seventeenth century. Jung, and his close associates after him, began formulating a living link between spirit and matter, an aspect of reality long rejected in our civilization. This hard-won, solid accomplishment and its evolution will occupy the discussion ahead.

11

**Subject and object**

Since Descartes, the Occident has cleaved the world in two. According to Descartes, there are thinking things (*res cogitans*) and extended things (*res extensa*), subjects and objects. For the Westerner there are subjects that perceive and there are objects that are perceived. The subject perceives the world and manipulates it as an object. The basic philosophical and scientific framework that explains the relationship between subjects and objects is thought to be causality. The subject is an agent and the actions of the subject cause an effect in or on an object outside the subject. Subjects make things happen in the world of objects. Subject and object, cause and effect, are elements of the Western world-view underlying everything we do. As Jungian psychology has shown, however, and as the following chapters will examine, this view of the world is not correct, or at least inadequate.

The experiences that I will be focusing on show that the division of life into subjective "inside" and objective "outside" does not fit our experience or the facts that emerge in the course of an analytic journey. Indeed, we will also discover that dividing the world into subject and object is not just a facile understanding of reality; it is a dangerous one. When we wish to alleviate past emotional pain in a genuine way, to clarify disorientations in the present and to live honestly and meaningfully into an uncertain future, the distinction between subject and object breaks down. Experiences that transpire in the course of an inner journey, such as depth analysis, show that at times what we think of as an object, the external material world, can also act as a subject. There are moments in life when we become the object of physical events in the external world that act, as a subject, on *us*.

An example will serve to clarify this shift.

A woman in analysis who was working on recovering her personal strength and learning to trust her emotions dreamed of bear claws. We discussed the dream in an analytic hour, and she realized that the bear claw represented her own strength, her own ability to give someone a swat, when she needed to protect herself and meet her needs. We also discussed the bear as an image of the mothering principle. The mother bear tends her cubs assiduously, fights any adversary to protect them and, when the cubs are old enough, unsentimentally leaves them to fend for themselves as adults in their new life. This is exactly the kind of mothering the woman did not receive, and the dream was showing her an image of caring, forceful and unsentimental attitudes which she could now develop in the course of her psychological work. Then, the day after the discussion of the bear claw dream, the woman went into a fabric store to buy some material for a project in her home. As she was standing in line to pay for the goods, she noticed the customer waiting in front of her had a large handful of buttons. Looking at the buttons more closely, the dreamer noticed that embossed on each button was the image of a bear claw.

The woman was struck by the appearance in outer reality of her dream image from a few nights before. The event drove home the message discussed just the previous day in her analytic hour and reinforced her resolve to continue developing her personal strength. She felt affirmed by the occurrence; it impressed a confirming and validating effect on her and on her wish to mature. It could have been dismissed as a chance event. But what are the chances! She was, instead, touched by the event and it sank into her; she let its impact work on her and affirm her struggle away from passivity and dependence.

In this instance an event in the material world acted on her is if it were a subject and she were the object. The event impressed a state of mind on her; her inner emotions and attitudes were affected by an outer event, just as if that event had been a person who said something to influence her. Whenever a so-called "outside" event behaves as an intelligent and message-bearing subject toward us, it appears that the outer world is not merely an "extended thing," but is in fact an agent in its own right. Whenever we experience subject and object reversed, and the material world acts in a meaningful way, there is a direct relationship between physical events and emotional growth. This relationship, this "road between matter and spirit," is at the heart of Jungian psychology. While every contemporary psychology that I am aware of focuses on the ego, the "I," on the subject, on the "doing" part of ourselves, Jung very early found that point of view wanting.

Since Freud, the focus of psychology has been on this "I." Problems in life are dissected as coming from distortions in the way that the ego experiences and makes choices. Clinical psychology says those distortions issue from events in the past by which the "I" has been misshapen and rendered unable to meet the demands of reality. Various schools understand the nature of those pressures in ways typical of their own assumptions: as stemming from sexuality, or power needs, or mothering, or separation or pride, for example. And the various schools all have procedures for overcoming the effect of these childhood errors. Some focus on the relationship between therapist and client, some on recovering memories, some on affective recognition, some on expressive modalities, some on thinking that is out of kilter, some on ritual replay, to cite a few instances. But Jung saw something else. He observed that when we go into ourselves—when we are swamped by what ails us, and when we consciously examine the storm inside—something starts happening in the outer world. Events in the outer, physical world itself come to us in moments of resonance, guidance and response. Something else, at times, populates occurrences in the material world, and its presence can have a very powerful effect on resolving the particular confusion besetting us.

Putting fact and experience before theory, Jung recognized that these events are of central importance in the process of healing. He perceived that our understanding of causality, and the time and space it works in, does not do justice to the capacity for healing that is inborn in every human being. Jung turned his attention relentlessly to this deeper dimension of life: to the fact that there is something else besides our actions going on in the world and that this something else has intelligence and intent which heals.

He realized that any serious inner work proceeds not only by the investigation of forces that have shaped our lives but also by an attunement to what the "outer" or "objective" world is doing to help heal us. How events cross our path and the significance of certain material or physical occurrences in the outer world occupy key analytic attention in Jungian work. It is as important to observe these happenings in the present as it is to evaluate and attempt to overcome past injuries and destructive pressures from the years behind us. It is not that Jungian work avoids delving into the painful and confusing questions of our origin; it is that without the convergence of something "outside" our subjective personality which operates independently of our own intentions, the full depth of the personality will not be reached. Even when the past has led to problems in our development, there is a creative present attempting to guide us into a fuller life. Understanding and knowing how to respond to this creative present is a crucial feature of Jungian work.

Jung was significantly helped in his inquiry into the nature of reality by one very important person, Nobel laureate Wolfgang Pauli. Pauli was among the handful of scientists instrumental in the development of quantum physics in 1927. I will be looking a great deal more at Pauli, the scope of his contributions and how they originated in his friendship and dialogue with Jung. Jung's work as a psychiatrist concerned the inner world of the human being; Pauli, as a nuclear physicist, was concerned with the laws governing events in the outer world. They both realized that certain moments along life's journey, where events in the outer, physical world come to meet an individual, defied many of their own discipline's assumptions. It is the physical world that responds psychologically in these moments.

The physical world is the work of the physicist. But how can physics admit that matter has meaning? The inner or psychological world is the work of the psychotherapist. And how does a psychologist conceptualize the fact that inner psychological processes occur externally in the material world? Both researchers knew that there was nothing in their individual points of view to explain these things and both researchers knew that their particular discipline addressed only part of life's picture since such occurrences involve both the inner psychological and outer physical worlds. Both knew that their respective viewpoints did not adequately formulate a view of nature's wholeness. The two men's challenge to each other concerning new facts and fresh points of view encouraged both pioneers to take a renewed look at the evidence. Their recognition of the strengths and weaknesses of their respective fields—and their mutual posing of difficult questions regarding the substance and fragility of the other's standpoint—is a fascinating narrative.

In the next generation, one of Jung's most articulate students, Marie-Louise von Franz, picked up the work the two men had begun, and she continued examining their points of view in the years after the deaths of Jung and Pauli. Well known as a trusted interpreter of Jung's work, she brought to their questions a thorough grounding in the theory and practice of Jungian psychology as well as a keen appreciation for the scientific questions that their discussions touched on. In addition to her close working relationship with Jung's ideas from the age of eighteen until her death sixty-five years later, she also maintained a special friendship with Pauli through the last years of his life. Von Franz's and Pauli's personal connection and enthusiastic discussions encompassed questions of theory and practice in Jungian psychology and in modern physics, the viewpoint of physics on psychology as well as the viewpoint of psychology on physics. The need for a broader point of view in reevaluating the relationship between "inner" and "outer" in both specialties was appreciated by each of them. Both intellectually and personally, von Franz was in a prime position to carry on the dialogue between the two men as well as to put it in a perspective accessible to subsequent generations. In addition to distilling and formulating the thought emerging between Jung and Pauli, von Franz's writings picked up its breadth and depth and examined it against additional backdrops: the Orient, number symbolism, biology, philosophy, mythology and the collapse of Christianity. Her contributions to building the road between matter and spirit will likewise occupy this book.

The road that Jung, Pauli and von Franz have prepared for us, and where it leads from here, is important not only to today's Jungians. The road between matter and spirit asks us to recognize intellectually and experience emotionally the full extent of Jung's inquiry into the nature of reality. A heart-felt relation to the nonrationality of the healing process, which at times meets us on the outside, is deeply significant for psychological growth. Considerations of "psychological dynamics," which are so pervasive in contemporary psychology, need to be examined in light of deeper experience. Finally, for both analyst and analysand, healing is less a matter of personality theory than of encountering the nonrational intensity that can shape life's direction. Jung uncovered a fundamentally new point of view that stands to inspire further research into the deeper nature of psychological healing.

**The chapters ahead**

Jung coined the word synchronicity to signify those events characterized by the inner and outer worlds acting in tandem with an emotional impact. A synchronicity is a meaningful coincidence between a dream or state of mind and an event in the outer, physical world.

Of course, a key feature of synchronicity is that it cannot be explained by causality. The event seems like chance or coincidence, and rationally one would be content to leave it at that, but this assessment does not do justice to the emotions that accompany the perception of the synchronicity. The coincidence wants to convey something. There is a meaning in it, waiting to be understood. The image from a dream appears in an outer physical event, external to us. We are touched, and from that opened position we want to understand.

Throughout this book, then, the meaningful relationship between our inner and outer worlds is explored. In the next chapter I shall discuss the phenomenon of synchronicity in more detail. I will compare its implications with those that have come out of quantum physics and elucidate how new perceptions of reality, both in the case of synchronicity and in the case of atomic physics, require us to reevaluate how we look at life. The relation between Jung and Pauli, as they probed these questions together, will also receive our attention.

The phenomenon of synchronicity challenges the concept of the archetype that Jung initially formulated in the first part of his life. Subsequently he reexplored this concept and with Pauli's help attempted a wider definition of his hypothesis. Chapter two examines the evolution of Jung's grasp of the archetype and also examines the connection between the archetype and matter.

Chapter three clarifies the matter-spirit relationship by considering a very prevalent image in Pauli's dreams, the Stranger. In this chapter I survey how the Stranger evolved over Pauli's life and how the Stranger dream-image personifies the unity of inner and outer, spirit and matter. By investigating characteristics of the Stranger image we will uncover features of the unitary reality he symbolizes, including his link to representations of Mercurius.

How is it that the inner world and the outer world converge at certain moments? That will be the spotlight of the fourth chapter. Jung and Pauli together posited that the link between these two domains of experience, which we have been taught to treat separately but which synchronicity shows to possess a secret symmetry, may be understood through the symbolism of numbers. Marie-Louise von Franz took up this idea in her writings after the deaths of Jung and Pauli, and it is to the psychology of numbers that we first turn in chapter four. Another attempt to grasp and conceptualize the road between matter and spirit is to be found in Jung's, Pauli's and particularly von Franz's writings on images of dual mandalas and of Sophia. These images are then interpreted as portraying the nature of reality which lies beneath subject and object and which informs them both.

Having lightly touched on the question of history in the previous chapter, I return to the historical point of view in the final chapter, examining Jung's understanding of the main dynamics of the last two thousand years of Western history. This will help us to place the split between matter and spirit in a larger context. It will also help us to appreciate the important challenge posed by the inadequacy of the prevailing Western view.

In the next chapter we shall begin by acquainting ourselves with the developments in physics and psychology at the beginning of the twentieth century. They paved the way for a new point of view.

# 1
# A New Century

Quantum physics and depth psychology were both born at the beginning of the twentieth century. It is no accident that these two fields came into existence at the same time. By investigating two of their main representatives, this chapter will explore the parallel understanding of nature that emerged simultaneously in these disciplines. So that we can appreciate the interchange between Wolfgang Pauli in quantum physics and C.G. Jung in depth psychology, an overview of their corresponding discoveries begins our inquiry into the dialogue between matter and spirit. First we will follow the development of quantum physics,[1] then the evolution of Jung's position, and then we will compare the two.

## The quantum

The 1927 foundation of quantum physics was carried out by a large team of young physicists, but three names stand out in these efforts which were finalized in Copenhagen: Niels Bohr, a Dane; Werner Heisenberg, a German; and, of course, the Austrian Wolfgang Pauli, who would eventually reside in Zürich. Their new theory of matter was called, appropriately, the Copenhagen Interpretation of Quantum Mechanics.[2]

---

[1] Quantum mechanics or quantum physics (terms used here interchangeably) investigates the mechanics or physical behavior of particles within the atom. The discovery of quantum physics provided insights into the workings of nature that overturned the assumptions of classical physics which had reigned since the time of their formulation by Isaac Newton in the seventeenth century.

[2] *Copenhagen*, a very interesting play by Michael Frayn, dealing with the relationship between two of these men, Bohr and Heisenberg, won three Tony awards in 2000 and was performed to packed houses around the country. It concerns a historically fictionalized account of the relation between Bohr and Heisenberg during World War Two when Bohr, living in Nazi-occupied Denmark, was in fact visited by Heisenberg, then director of the Nazi atomic bomb project.

At some point in our education we have probably learned about Newton and his famous formula F = MA, meaning that force equals mass times acceleration. This was a causally-based understanding of the actions and reactions between two objects in the physical world. The classic example is of one pool ball striking another pool ball. If you know the mass and the velocity of the first ball, and you know the mass of the second, you can predict the resulting motion of the second when the first strikes it. This is an example of the causality and predictability so dear to science up until about 1900: one event initiates another event, and the result of the interaction can be calculated mathematically.

However, that understanding started to fall apart at the end of the nineteenth century. Cracks appearing in Newton's seventeenth-century edifice can be traced back to 1895 as a rough starting point.[3] At that time J.J. Thomson in England discovered the electron. The inner structure of the atom had begun to occupy the attention of scientists, and smaller particles within the atom were about to be explored. It was clear that the investigation of the subatomic world was the next frontier for physical science. In 1900 a German researcher, Max Planck, posed further questions that took physicists twenty-seven years to answer. It was known from investigating the heat radiation of hot pieces of metal that experimental results and theoretical predictions did not quite match. Facts did not fit theory.

---

No one knows the content of their discussion, but whatever happened, the friendship between the two men never recovered after this meeting. It is surmised that Heisenberg approached Bohr on matters of building the Nazi atomic bomb and that Bohr, a European humanist to the core, hotly refused. Michael Frayn's play conveys a very engaging interchange of personality and a feeling for the times. The play also does an admirable job of explaining the basic principles of quantum physics. It is available on DVD from PBS. The warm reception given the play indicates that the themes we are discussing here are ready to be entertained by the general public, and that once again Jung's work has anticipated developments in collective consciousness by fifty to a hundred years.

[3] The following account of quantum physics owes much to Robert H. March, *Physics for Poets*, chaps. 14-15. I highly recommend it.

Planck then reexamined the suppositions of classical physics from which the calculations had been made. One of those assumptions from Newton's theory was that energy can exist in any amount whatsoever. It was thought that there can be a little bit of energy, a little more energy, a little bit more energy, and so on. But Planck found that energy does not work like that. Energy exists in discrete units or specific chunks, not in any possible gradation. As an analogy, previous to Planck energy levels in nature were taken to be like the sound of a trombone, sliding smoothly up the scale, existing in any possible progression. But in fact energy is like a trumpet on which only certain discrete notes can be played. Energy does not slide between values, it hops. Or, to give another picture: the discovery of Planck says, by analogy, that it is as if your car could be at rest, and then it could go five miles an hour, then ten miles an hour, fifteen miles an hour, but it could never go twelve-and-a-half miles an hour: energy exists in steps (figure 1), while classical physics says energy is continuous (figure 2). In other words, classical physics held that energy could gradually increase in a smooth way while Planck discovered that energy increases in regular increments.

We do not have to worry about numbers and mathematics here, but these jumps increase step-by-step by an amount called the *quantum,* which is defined by a numerical value called Planck's constant. This teensy little piece or quantum or step of energy is the building block of higher energy levels. It is a very tiny amount of energy, and energy can only exist in multiples of that quantity. It is so small compared to the total energy in large, ball-like interactions that it can go unnoticed at the levels of large-sized objects: that is, effects of the discrete multiples of the quantum value are only really measurable at small, subatomic levels. There was, though, no place in Newton's framework for the concept of discrete energy units. Planck's discovery was utterly revolutionary.

In 1905, Einstein's theory of special relativity was developed. This is another branch of physics, but I mention it in order to place quantum physics within the history of science.

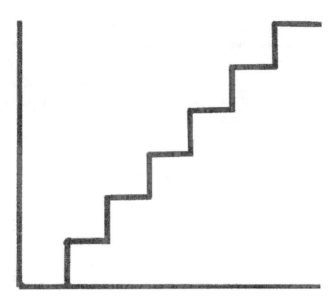

Figure 1. Quantum physics' representation of energy.

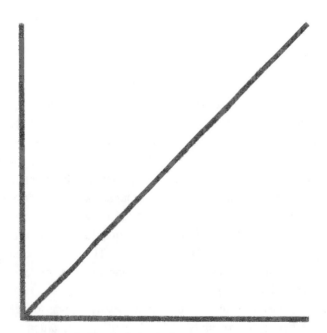

Figure 2. Classical physics' representation of energy.

How did this quantum innovation contribute to the discoveries into the nature of the atom which Pauli and others uncovered? The story continues in 1911. Enter Ernest Rutherford, a New Zealander working in England and eventually settling in Canada. Rutherford showed for the first time that the atom has a very tiny core of intensely concentrated matter at its center, called the nucleus. The discovery of this nucleus is a remarkable achievement. If we visualize the atom to be the size of a football field (100 yards), then the nucleus would be at the fifty-yard line and would be the size of a postage stamp.[4]

Next, in 1913, Niels Bohr, who would head up the Copenhagen team, made the daring hypothesis that the atom is shaped like a solar system, with electrons orbiting around the intensely concentrated nucleus Rutherford had found (figure 3).

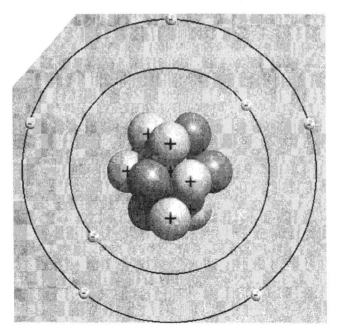

Figure 3. Artist's conception of atom with nucleus and electrons.

---

[4] See Brian Sweeney and Jacqueline Owens, "Ernest Rutherford: Atom Man.".

Bohr then came upon the very unexpected discovery that the electrons circled around the nucleus of the atom in very specific energy levels consisting of whole-number multiples of a minute amount of energy. This energy level could be one times this tiny energy level, two times and so on—never one-half or one-and-a-half times this small level. And the value of this tiny energy level turned out tobe exactly Planck's constant!

Picture the solar system model where the electrons have successive orbits away from the nucleus as planets have successive orbits away from the sun. Electrons in the orbit closest to the nucleus will have an energy level of one times Planck's constant. Electrons in the next successive orbit will have a value of two times Planck's constant. There can never be an orbit with an electron that has an energy value one-and-a-half times Planck's constant. Bohr saw that electrons follow the energy limitation of Planck and that the orbits of the electrons around the nucleus are all multiples of that basic number. Once again energy is discontinuous. There is no continuum of energy gradation in heat radiation or in the electrons of an atom. As Planck's constant applies to heat radiation, so it also applies to energy levels of electrons in the atom. As there is nothing in classical physics to explain the laws of heat radiation, so there is nothing in classical physics to explain the workings of the electrons in the atom. Planck's discovery was confirmed in 1913: nature comes with a sort of built-in regularity. This is something I will return to as Jung, Pauli and von Franz try to understand that there is an inborn mathematical structure to the universe. There are certain "just so" amounts of energy. The world is simply built that way.

To again place where we are in the history of physics, note that in 1915 Einstein elaborated on his theory of relativity. That is not directly related to the Copenhagen research concerning the nature of the inner workings of the atom, but it might be helpful to recognize how the atomic research fits into developments in physics as a whole. Einstein's work concerned motion in nature on the scale of the solar system while our discussion relates to the inner workings of the atom. Einstein was in contact with the researchers working on the atom, although he never agreed with them concerning their final interpretations. The dialogue between Einstein and the Copenhagen group is an intriguing story on its own account, but it is outside the scope of this book.

Back to the atom. The line of research starting with Thomson and Rutherford, then picked up by Bohr's group, came to fruition in that memorable year 1927. The understanding of how electrons in the atom function and the mathematical formulas that describe exactly how they behave were finalized after fourteen years of effort.

**A new kind of motion**

There is an additional discovery of the Copenhagen group that later held particular weight for Jung. The quantum revolution recognized not only that there were distinct quantities of energy at the heart of matter but also that there was a new principle or pattern of motion in the way subatomic particles moved. The electron, once energized from without, follows a trajectory that cannot be anticipated by any causal methods. The old views of Newton were useless once again.

The Copenhagen group was struck by a particular property of light. When a scientist heats a container filled with a gas to a high temperature, or energizes the gas electrically, it will start to glow. Think of a neon light. If the light that comes out of the tube is passed through a strong prism, it will be resolved into a few bands of specific colors. We have all played with a prism as children and have seen the rainbow shine out of its one side when held up to the sun: the prism breaks up the mixture of colors in the glow of sunlight into a rainbow of colors. Similarly scientists can put the light that comes off a heated gas through a very precise prism and see exactly each of the discrete colors that exist within it. As they very precisely separate out the specifically colored bands of light from the gas, they reveal distinct patterns called spectral lines (Figures 4 and 5, next page). Each line is a very accurately delineated color.

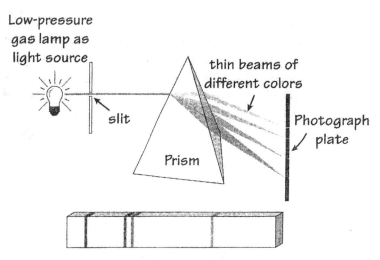

Figure 4. Apparatus for producing spectral lines.

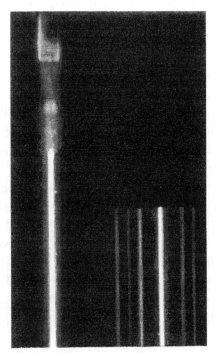

Figure 5. Excited tube of helium gas (left) with its spectral lines.

The color of light is determined by its wavelength, by how fast the electro-magnetic field is vibrating. This means that if a light can be broken up into, say, three spectral lines, there are three different frequencies of electro-magnetic vibration making up the light coming from the atom in the gas. These values are always the same for a particular element. A gas of a different element will yield a different pattern of light colors, a different collection of discrete frequencies of light; in other words, a different set of spectral lines.

The energy levels of the electrons' orbits account for this phenomenon. When energy is added to the gas from heat or electricity and an activated electron moves up to the next orbit's energy level, it is unstable at that point, so it falls back to its previous orbit. When it falls back to its original state, the extra energy that it had acquired is then emitted as light. If more energy is added, the electron will jump up to a still higher orbit, and the increased energy that is emitted when it falls back will be exhibited as a different color of light. Still more energy, yet a different color of light, and so on. The frequency or color of the light is dependent on the amount of energy "distance" between the two electron levels at different orbits.

But significantly, when an atom is energized *it cannot be predicted* whether any given electron in it will traverse, for example, from one orbit to another by going from its home orbit to a higher orbit level directly or by stopping along the way at intermediate orbits (Figure 6, next page). As the energy of the electrons in the atoms starts to decrease, and the electrons fall back to their original lower energy orbit, it cannot be predicted whether a particular electron will go directly from its temporary higher orbit to its regular lower state or whether it will pass through intermediate orbits along the way. The colors radiated by the electron will be different, depending on its path of movement back to its original orbit. This is how scientists were able to "see" the individual movements of electrons. And the remarkable observation was that *the course that the electron follows from one orbit to another, and thus the light that it emits, cannot be known from what excited it to move.* Maybe the excited electron will go between its highest and lowest orbits directly and emit one color of light when its energy decreases. Or maybe it will go from its high to low orbit through an intermediate step or steps and emit two or more colors of light. The motion of an electron is always an independent, undetermined motion. This kind of motion, a motion not definable by its cause, was a revolutionary discovery. It defied the principle of causality on which classical physics is based.

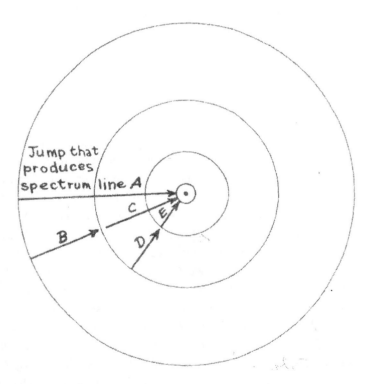

Figure 6. Electron jumps that produce spectral lines.

Bohr, Heisenberg, and Pauli calculated the exact amount of energy in each electron orbit by observing the spectral lines of light emitted from a heated gas. This means that all the electrons of all the atoms in the gas on average move between orbits in predictable ways, emitting the typical spectral lines for that gas. But the actual motion of any single electron in an excited atom remains unpredictable. While classical physics can predict motion from a cause, the quantum physicists saw that single motions at the subatomic level have a trajectory of their own.

Wolfgang Pauli was so important to Jung because he was one of the key physicists that participated in the world-view shift that broke all the assumptions of classical physics. The independent movement of the electron, undetermined by what set it in motion, would remind Jung of the independent psychological movement that characterizes moments of healing. The discovery of a new kind of motion in quantum mechanics concerning the nature of physical reality is exactly paralleled by Jung's research into the spontaneous nature of the healing process which occurs along the psychological journey. Both disciplines identified a new kind of motion undetermined by causality. The similarity between the paradigm shift in science coming out of quantum physics and the paradigm shift in psychology coming out of Jung's discovery is remarkable.

**The players**

See the next three pages for photos of Jung and Pauli and a time-line chart of their lives (Figures 7, 8, 9).

A survey of the personal lives of Jung and Pauli, to understand not only what they accomplished and when, but also to see how they contributed to the other's growth, will add a personal dimension to their ideas. Since both men recognized similarities among the conclusions they were reaching from research in their respective fields, it will be instructive to examine their lives to see the overlap both in terms of a personal friendship and the interchange of ideas. Their fertile dialogue concerning the evolving research into the nature of atoms in the outer material world and

Figure 7. Portrait of C.G. Jung.

Figure 8. Portrait of Wolfgang Pauli.

| C.G. Jung | | Wolfgang Pauli |
|---|---|---|
| 1875 | born in NE Switzerland: I | |
| 1900 | finishes medical school in Basel | born in Vienna |
| | starts psychiatric residency in Zürich | |
| 1907 | meets Sigmund Freud | |
| 1913 | collaboration with Freud ends | |
| | begins "night sea journey:" II | (Bohr postulates quantum orbits) |
| 1918 | | begins university studies in Münich |
| 1921 | | receives Ph.D.; goes to Göttingen |
| 1922 | | to Physics Institute in Hamburg |
| 1922-23 | | with Niels Bohr in Copenhagen |
| 1925 | | the Pauli exclusion principle |
| 1927 | | Copenhagen Interpretation of QM |
| 1928 | receives *Secret of the Golden Flower* | moves to Zürich; ETH professor |
| | comes out of the darkness: III | marriage; divorce; personal collapse |
| 1932 | begins correspondence with Pauli | consults with Jung |
| 1933 | | gets back on his feet |
| 1940-46 | | wartime in Princeton; refuses Los Alamos |
| 1945 | | Nobel prize; depressed over US science |
| 1946 | | returns to Zürich; new dream interest |
| 1944 | heart attack: IV | |
| 1944-56 | major writing: (*Psychology and Alchemy* [1944], *Psychology of the Transference* [1946], *Aion* [1951], "Synchronicity" [1952], *Answer to Job* [1952], *Mysterium Coniunctions* [1955-56]) | |
| 1952 | | Kepler essay |
| 1958 | | dies in Zürich |
| 1961 | dies in Küsnacht | |

Fig. 9. Time-line of Jung and Pauli.

the healing process within the inner world takes on an added poignancy when viewed against the contours of their lives.

Four main periods make up the life and work of Carl Jung.

The first period is from the time he was born in northeast Switzerland in 1875 until the end of his relationship with Freud. That is the period during which he received his education, became a medical doctor and then a psychiatrist, and when he learned the psychoanalytic method. He partly developed his understanding of psychological treatment on his own as a young psychiatric resident in Zürich and partly learned from Freud some basics of the psychological approach which he built upon subsequently.

Jung met Freud in 1907. Freud taught him an enormous amount and gave Jung confidence that he was on the right track with his basic understanding of many psychological concepts. It was very supportive for Jung to hear that another practitioner had independently come to conclusions similar to his own. Their friendship continued until 1913, when the collaboration ended. Freud's being an atheist and Jung's rejection of the godless position surely had something to do with it. Jung found Freud's secular point of view at first stimulating in its empiricism but eventually he felt that it was too narrow to encompass the complexity of factors that make up a full life.

The year 1913 begins a second phase of Jung's life, lasting to 1928. By 1913 Jung had become a doctor, a psychiatrist and a psychoanalyst. But he was no longer able to agree with Freud's causal and atheistic outlook. Yet, since the conclusions Freud had reached meant much to Jung, the years after the break with Freud were very difficult. Imagine the situation in Europe during this time: a repressive provincialism held over from Victorian moralism reigned supreme. Jung in Zürich and Freud in Vienna were working separately in this constraining atmosphere, recognizing and trying to qualify and quantify those irrational-seeming factors that are the motivators for all we do. It was terribly lonely work. For each to have come across another, working independently and with conclusions not dissimilar to his own, was consequential to both.

Jung gratefully acknowledged Freud's contributions to his own outlook.[5] Likewise, C.A. Meier, a close associate of Jung who studied medicine in Vienna in the 1920s and was part of Freud's small psychoanalytic group there,[6] told me in a personal conversation that Freud would continually ask him, "How is Jung? How is Jung?" That the breakup was very painful for both men is clear. Jung lost a treasured support, particularly so since Freud was a generation older than Jung and had years more consulting-room experience. Even though Jung may not have agreed with all of Freud's conclusions, he had based some of his views on therapy from his discussions with Freud. With the loss of his connection to Freud, Jung also lost a teacher and a point of orientation.

The break with Freud cost Jung fifteen years of disorientation as he struggled to define and clarify his own ideas to the point where he felt they were ready to be shared with colleagues and students. The period between 1913 and 1928 was Jung's "night sea journey," a time of despair and searching. He did not give up his involvement in the outer world, although he did resign from a lectureship at the University of Zürich, and he pulled back his stake in public life. He remained a psychiatrist and devoted father, but with a reduced investment in other, outer activities; and he began to examine his own inner processes. These fifteen years were a very long psychological pregnancy.

Until 1928, Jung carefully observed and recorded his own dreams and fantasies, studied the same in his patients, and scanned the corpus of world mythology for parallels to the dream images he was seeing. It is during this time that he discovered the inner psychological process, previously undocumented—the inborn acausal psychological healing process. In contrast to Freud, who thought that we are born *tabula rasa* (empty slates) and who held that psychological healing was a matter of recovering forcefully

---

[5] See "The 'Face to Face' Interview," in William McGuire, ed., *C.G. Jung Speaking*, pp. 424ff.

[6] Meier was also the first president of the C.G. Jung Institute in Zurich when it was founded in 1948.

forgotten experiences, Jung had found a wider horizon. As Jung watched himself gain ground in finding a new point of view for his psychological work, and a new inner confidence in that work and in his life, he began his life-long documentation of the process that tries to put us back together when we lose our bearings—if we know how to cooperate with it. This was the birth from those fifteen, difficult psychologically pregnant years of 1913 to 1928.

Jung had seen the healing process at work in himself and in his patients, and then he asked himself, "Is this culturally determined or have I come upon something common to all humanity?"

The year 1928 was a singular one in Jung's life. He received a translation of a Chinese Taoist text that describes the process of meditation and enlightenment in exactly the same metaphor that he had established for the process of healing. The text came from a German missionary to China, Richard Wilhelm, who, by the way, liked to say that he never baptized a single Chinese. Jung called receiving this text "one of the most significant events of my life," and of Wilhelm he said, "it seems to me as if I had received more from him than from any other man."[7] Wilhelm, a devoted Sinologist and lover of China and Chinese culture, used his time there to build a bridge between Western understanding and the Chinese mind; he learned from the Chinese, and did not try to convert them. Wilhelm is more commonly known as the man who brought the *I Ching* from China to the West and provided us with its first coherent translation.

The text Wilhelm sent to Jung was called *The Secret of the Golden Flower*.[8] The oral tradition probably originated in the eighth century AD, though the text Wilhelm sent Jung dates from woodcuts of the seventeenth century.[9] Similarities in the pattern of illustrations in the text to those he had found in his inner self-

---

[7] "Richard Wilhelm: In Memoriam," *The Spirit in Man, Art, and Literature*, CW 15, par. 96. [CW refers throughout to C.G. Jung, *The Collected Works*]

[8] Jung's commentary appears in *Alchemical Studies,* CW 13, pars. 1ff.

[9] C.G. Jung and Richard Wilhelm, *The Secret of the Golden Flower.*

examination are what gave Jung the courage to say that he had found a process in human nature that is inborn and transcultural. The dynamic he had watched in himself and in his patients was also illustrated in an Eastern text. Its presence in two widely differing cultures, West and East, suggested that it is not something imbibed from any cultural system, but rather is inherently within and exists in everybody irrespective of cultural background. Naturally, its noncausal character had struck Jung forcibly.

By 1928 Jung's confusion and disorientation had come to an end and he had surfaced after his night sea journey with a completely new point of view which became the cornerstone of Jungian psychology. He no longer relied on what he had learned from Freud and had something of incredible value to put in its place. A new, third phase of his life had begun.

From 1928 to 1944 Jung refined and published his newly-won and fundamental insight, while continuing to observe how it worked in his own life and in his patients. This third phase of his life could be called his nuts and bolts period. To develop his elegantly simple observation that there is a purposive, inborn healing process, he studied all the mythological texts at his disposal. As his basic ideas were pretty much clear by 1928, he subsequently worked at authenticating and developing those findings for the next sixteen years, examining tens of thousands of dreams to clarify and confirm his hypothesis, while studying myths to corroborate similar patterns.

The central mythological system with a reservoir of images that helped illuminate the pattern Jung was investigating was medieval alchemy.[10] During this part of his life Jung's efforts went into

---

[10] The origins of alchemy can be traced back to Hellenistic Egypt. After the collapse of the empires of antiquity, it found safe haven in Arabic culture until returning from there to medieval Europe. Alchemists, sort of "pre-chemists," literally tried to turn some worthless piece of material into gold or another precious substance. They cooked, chopped, baked and prayed, recording their recipes in the symbolic language of a prescientific mind. Jung studied their writings as metaphors to understand how the psyche tries to heal itself through transforming

documenting mythological schema that could provide varied images of the healing process in all its facets. His writings attempted to establish what the psychological process of healing is, how it works and what symbols it uses. He took pains to describe his observations in detail and to communicate those facts in a fashion accessible to sympathetic minds. That made up the purpose of Jung's work until 1944 when he was 69.

In 1944, beginning the final phase of his life, Jung had a heart attack and nearly died. After a series of near-death experiences— themselves a beautiful document of the soul that is described in his autobiography—he realized that his life was indeed not finished.[11] In his near-death visions, he heard himself being called back to earth, and reluctantly he decided to return. Thus from 1944 to his death in 1961 he felt he had a second lease on life. In this phase he decided to describe his findings just as the material dictated, not as the needs of a reader might warrant. So he did not write his last works with the reader in mind, as he had done previously—which is why these last works are relatively difficult to understand; rather his last works were written with the integrity of the material in mind. In his final writings he did not care about the audience as much as he cared about the demands of the material. So the real guts of Jung came out in his writing after 1944: this is the period of his major authorship. The period of active research into his basic hypothesis had started when Jung was 53 in 1928; his final period began when he was 69. It was also during this last period that Wolfgang Pauli played an important part in Jung's creative development.[12]

---

the difficult part of our personality into something of value and sustenance—through the inner healing process, in other words. Both the alchemists' imagining the goings-on in the piece of material they thought they were transforming and Jung's observing the goings-on in a psychologically transforming personality evidenced the creative, goal-oriented process of fragmentation and recentering.

[11] *Memories, Dreams, Reflections*, chap. 10.

[12] Those works include *Psychology and Alchemy* (1944, CW 12), "The Psychology of the Transference" (1946, in *The Practice of Psychotherapy*, CW 16), *Aion*

That is Jung. Now Pauli.[13]

Wolfgang Pauli, twenty-five years younger than Jung, was born in Vienna in 1900. His father was Jewish, but Pauli was raised Catholic. He did not know of his Jewish ancestry until someone in graduate school pointed out to him that his face possessed Jewish features.[14] He began to ask questions and found out that his father had converted to Catholicism. It was much easier for a non-Jew to make professional progress in nineteenth-century Vienna than it was for a Jew. His father was a professor of medical chemistry in Vienna, a position he could not have gained as a Jew. Pauli converted to Judaism in adulthood.

In Vienna Pauli attended the *gymnasium*, which in the European system is attended by students aiming for higher education. He entered university in 1918 in München, earning his Ph.D. in 1921. He then took up a teaching position in Hamburg and spent a year (Fall 1922 to Fall 1923) at Niels Bohr's soon-to-be famous institute in Copenhagen. Pauli mostly lived and worked in Hamburg during the subsequent years but traveled back and forth between Copenhagen and Hamburg, until the Copenhagen interpretation of quantum mechanics was finalized.

Observe for a moment that—almost to the year—during the exact same period that Jung was cooped up in his night sea journey from 1913 to 1928, discovering the psychology of a basic principle of human nature, the science of quantum mechanics, which itself documented revolutionary new facts of physical nature, was in the

---

(1951, CW 9i), "Synchronicity: An Acausal Connecting Principle" (1952, in *The Structure and Dynamics of the Psyche*, CW 8 ), "Answer to Job" (1952, in *Psychology and Religion*, CW 11) and *Mysterium Coniunctionis* (1955-56, CW 14).)

[13] Sources for Pauli's life are: Abraham Pais, "Wolfgang Pauli," *The Genius of Science*, chap. 11; Charles P. Enz, *No Time To Be Brief: A Scientific Biography of Wolfgang Pauli* and *Pauli hat gesagt: Eine Biographie des Nobel-preisträgers Wolfgang Pauli, 1900-1958;* and David Lindorff, *Pauli and Jung: The Meeting of Two Great Minds.*

[14] See Herbert van Erkelens, *Wolfgang Pauli und der Geist der Materie,* pp. 13f.

process of being discovered and formulated. These fourteen or fifteen years were vitally creative in two different cities and in two different disciplines; two different aspects of a single new world-view were in the process of birth, Through teamwork, the new viewpoint in physics began with Bohr's first atomic model and ended in Copenhagen. Its psychological parallel began with Jung's split from Freud and became largely finalized, at least in theory, with Jung's receiving the *Secret of the Golden Flower* from Richard Wilhelm. The physics model, though, is more than just a model of physics; it is a whole new way of looking at processes in nature. Likewise, Jung's psychological theory is more than just another way of understanding people; it reflects the same new comprehension of reality. A new principle of nature—of physical nature and of our psychological nature—was coming to consciousness separately and simultaneously. Pauli and Jung would have a lot to talk about.

Pauli, having finished the work on quantum mechanics, took up a professorship in 1928 at the Zürich ETH (Federal Institute of Technology), the MIT of German-speaking Switzerland. The post Pauli assumed was chair of theoretical physics. Einstein had already taught at the Zürich ETH after his discovery of the relativity theories, so it was well known in physics circles around the world, and Pauli's position was a coveted one. Pauli remained in that position until his death in 1958.

In 1932, just a few years after moving to Zürich, Pauli was in a personal crisis. He had married in Zürich, but it was clear early on that the union was wrong. Soon he found himself in divorce proceedings. He started drinking and getting into bar fights; certainly this was no way for a Herr Professor at the ETH to behave. He went to Jung seeking help. Jung told him that his problem was his relationship to women and referred him to a female analyst. Pauli worked with the woman for about six months. Her name, Erna Rosenbaum, is not well known today. Pauli found his footing in less than a year and remarried shortly thereafter. He also saw Jung for more analytic work after he had concluded with

Rosenbaum. Following that, the two men slowly began a professional friendship and personal dialogue.

From 1932 onward they maintained a lively correspondence, much of it edited by C.A. Meier and published under the title *Atom and Archetype*. Until nearly the end of Pauli's life in 1958 they discussed their common passion.

By 1940 the war in Europe was taking shape. Pauli, being half Jewish, was advised to flee in case the Nazis invade Switzerland. Zürich is not far from the Swiss-German border where Nazi tanks were amassing for such a possible invasion. He had an Austrian passport, a country under Nazi annexation, which would have made him subject to the Nazi command if the Nazis had advanced into Zürich. He fled to the United States and took up a position at the Institute for Advanced Studies in Princeton, where Einstein was also in residence. He stayed there throughout the war.

Although the atomic bomb was being created in Los Alamos during the time Pauli was in Princeton, he did not take part in the efforts. He was the only nuclear physicist to refuse to work on the so-called Manhattan project. Even though many of those working on the bomb had been his students, among them its leader Robert Oppenheimer, Pauli felt it was not the business of science to engineer mass destruction.

While in Princeton, Pauli was thoroughly distressed at the knowledge of the bomb's detonation; he fell into a deep depression and began having outbursts of rage. He said that he felt like he was living in a criminal atmosphere. He left Princeton in 1946 after the war was over, turning down a lucrative research position at the Institute for Advanced Studies, and he went back to Zürich to resume his work at the ETH. He returned to Switzerland realizing that the quantum mechanics he had helped create was responsible, at least partly, for mass murder.

In Zürich, Pauli was depressed and despairing. Feeling that he was effectively at the center of developments that eventually led to genocide, with Jung's help Pauli turned back to his dreams to try to understand the reaction from his unconscious to the travesty of two thermonuclear catastrophes. He consulted Jung not so much because his life was in a personal mess, but because he was so greatly distressed about what his beloved science had participated in. He put the question to his unconscious: What has gone wrong? How is it that our beloved science, created by spunky graduate students between games of ping-pong, has led to Hiroshima and Nagasaki?

We are distanced from the horror of nuclear holocaust today, since so many of us were born after World War Two. We easily forget its omnipresent threat, particularly given the terrorism of Islamic fundamentalism, which currently dominates our attention. The development of nuclear power in Iran and North Korea may change that, but for the moment we are more worried about localized explosions than those of world-destroying power.

The poignancy of the nuclear question, however, remains fresh in my mind due to an experience I had while serving in the Peace Corps in South Korea in the early seventies. I was on the faculty of a teacher-training college in a small town, and the chairman of my department was at Hiroshima when the bomb went off. Koreans had been conscripted into the Japanese army, so my Korean colleague found himself in a Japanese uniform driving a jeep away from Hiroshima on that fateful day. He told me that the shockwave from the blast blew him out of the vehicle, head first over the top of its windshield. And then that awful thunder. He recounted how he was part of the first clean-up crew to return to the bombed-out city. He said you cannot imagine what it was like reaching to grasp a child's outstretched arm, only to have the flesh from the arm peal away in your hand. Koreans are a physically tough lot and not easily given to expressing emotions. But when my boss told me that story he sobbed convulsively. He said it was an irony that twenty-five years previous he and I would have been the bitterest of enemies, and now here we were sitting together on a warm Saturday afternoon in the gentle breeze of an Oriental country summer, drinking a beer together. I will not forget him saying, "For God's sake, there must be no more Hiroshimas. Promise me there will be no more Hiroshimas."

Were the bombs dropped to end the war, because the bomb project itself had become an unstoppable machine or because the United States wanted to position itself in the upcoming cold war stand-off with Russia? The military, political and moral questions concerning the nuclear end of World War Two will probably be debated forever. But these questions were not the ones moving Pauli. He had been touched by the human tragedy that the Korean professor imbedded so forcefully in my memory. This was the care that had invaded Pauli, and he was deeply unhappy. The cause of his suffering is something we too would do well to remember.

Sickened in his heart with the consequences of what he had helped create, Pauli sought the reaction of his dreams. How would they conceive of the nuclear danger? How might they illuminate the threat of destruction? How would they regard the diabolical side of science? Pauli turned inside to investigate his dreams' symbolic expression of these problems and to seek their portrayal of a solution to what was occupying him. He inquired how his unconscious would react to the beginning of the nuclear age when the demonic power drive unleashed by science had become espoused to ethnic and national hatreds. In what way would dreams represent both the genesis and the solution of the atomic danger, and what could be learned from their message? These were his questions.

For the next fifteen years Pauli dreamed of the backdrop of the nuclear problem and discussed many of his dreams with Jung. Sometimes they would discuss matters in correspondence, sometimes in the consulting room and sometimes over dinner or at Jung's secluded tower-retreat in Bollingen along the Lake of Zürich, where Jung did much of his writing. About forty or fifty dreams were recorded during that time, and they have just been published, only in German so far, by Herbert van Erkelens.[15] A sampling of them has also been published in English in *Atom and*

---

[15] *Wolfgang Pauli und der Geist der Materie.*

*Archetype*, but the van Erkelens volume is more complete. Themes from these dreams will be discussed here in subsequent chapters.

Pauli continued working on this issue until 1958, when he collapsed while lecturing at the ETH and passed away in hospital in Zürich shortly thereafter of pancreatic cancer.

There is another detail worth mentioning. In 1952 Pauli wrote an essay on the astronomer Johannes Kepler (1571-1630).[16] Kepler was important to Pauli because Kepler's work shows up in the history of science just about the time the rational, empirical method of modern science took hold and the magical thinking of alchemy died out. Pauli was very curious to understand what was going on in scientists' minds and souls when science was born historically and as the magical thinking of the medieval era was dissolved. This essay will occupy part of the final chapter here.

Marie-Louise von Franz (Figure 10, next page), then, in taking up the dialogue between Pauli and Jung after their deaths, most directly continued their work. She was born in 1915 in München, so she was forty years Jung's, and fifteen years Pauli's, junior. She moved to Switzerland when she was three years old and was eighteen when she met Jung. There is as of 2006 no published biography of von Franz, so we have to rely on statements by and about her throughout the literature. She met Jung for the first time when invited to Bollingen, along with a group of university students, to spend the day and to talk with Jung in a relaxed atmosphere. He made a vivid impression on her,[17] and she then began to attend Jung's lectures at the ETH. Jung recognized her immediately, approached her with a warm greeting, and the two began a friendship which lasted until the end of Jung's life. Von Franz began analysis with him and repaid Jung for it by researching Greek and Latin alchemical texts. A Classics major at the University of Zürich, she helped Jung by translating the texts he

---

[16] "The Influence of Archetypal Ideas on the Scientific Theories of Kepler," in Pauli, *Writings on Physics and Philosophy*, pp. 244ff.

[17] See von Franz, "Bollingen, September 1982," a video interview.

Figure 10. Portrait of Marie-Louise von Franz.

was studying concerning the nature of mythological images that occur in dreams during the process of psychological healing. She was twenty-five when she finished her Ph.D., subsequently teaching Greek and Latin at the *gymnasium* in Küsnacht, the suburb of Zürich where Jung lived. Eventually she began a practice as a Jungian analyst, becoming one of the foremost interpreters of Jung's work for subsequent generations. Her generous, down-to-earth, keen-witted, emotionally accessible and fantastically creative personal style is something her students very much loved and will always remember.[18]

In addition to her friendship with Jung, von Franz maintained a relationship with Pauli. They shared their papers for mutual critique and discussed matters of physics and psychology as well as each other's dreams. She was certainly the person most suited to pick up the dialogue between Pauli and Jung. Her main works devoted to this theme and to carrying on their dialogue are *On Divination and Synchronicity* (1969 lectures published in 1980); *Number and Time* (1970); and *Projection and Recollection in Jungian Psychology* (1978). Her collected papers on this subject matter were published as *Psyche and Matter* (1992). Her activities during her last years were severely limited by Parkinson's disease, and she died at the age of 83 in 1998.

**Trajectory and meaning**

We have observed that just as an energized electron inside the atom follows a course of its own, so a synchronistic happening points forward in life in a completely unique manner. Our closer look into the atom has revealed that the excited electron seeks an endpoint not established by its cause; likewise, a synchronistic experience points to a development in our life unfettered by determinism. Both in the atom and in a synchronicity we have seen a trajectory, a movement toward a final point; in both cases the activity is headed somewhere.

---

[18] See Emmanuel Kennedy Zypolitas, ed., *The Fountain of the Love of Wisdom: An Homage to Marie-Louise von Franz*.

This trajectory needs closer scrutiny. Obviously it has to do with meaning in the case of a synchronicity because of the psychological message the moment communicates. Can the same thing be said about the trajectory of an electron? Can meaning be applied to that movement? Jung was initially inclined to say that it could while Pauli felt that it could not. In the end, Jung changed his mind.[19] The unpredictability of matter is, of course, what makes synchronicity possible. Since not all processes in nature follow predictable laws, there is unpredictability within the atom, and the same uncertainty opens the door to synchronicity. But this does not necessarily mean that the meaning in the movement of synchronicity also applies to movement at the subatomic level. The acausal and trajectory parallels do hold between the motion within an atom and in a synchronicity, though the question of meaning can be left open in the case of acausality at the subatomic level. However much the microphysical movement of the electron has to do with the psychological movement of synchronicity, their analogous relationship might end at the question of meaning. In this regard, synchronicity seems to be a completely unique phenomenon.

Two additional examples will assist in further elucidating the trajectory of nature and the meaning synchronicity brings to it.

The first vignette describes the most dramatic synchronistic event I have ever witnessed. It comes from a forty-year-old married woman in analysis. The second is from an experience of my own at the end of my training in Zürich. Both examples will illustrate

---

[19] Pauli wrote to Jung (November 1950): "I have grave misgivings about placing physical discontinuities and synchronicity on the same level . . . . I do, however, feel that although it cannot be proved, it can be argued that acausality in microphysics is a sort of 'preliminary stage' for your concept of 'synchronicity.' " (Meier, ed., *Atom and Archetype*, p. 56 and n. 5) The discontinuous or unpredictable "jumping" of the electron, in Pauli's view, is the same type of acausal motion found in a synchronicity and is the principle of nature that makes synchronicity possible, though it does not involve meaning as does synchronicity. Jung was convinced by Pauli's argument. Jung to Pauli (January 1951): "I fully agree with you that the synchronicity of the psychic sphere must be conceptually separated from the discontinuities of microphysics." (Ibid., p. 69)

another aspect of purposive and meaningful motion, as well as provide an opportunity to ask a further question concerning the composition of physical and psychological reality, that is, this intersection of the outer world with our inner psychology manifesting in dreams, images and emotions.

My analysand told of falling in love for the first time when she was sixteen. Her mother blew up and said to her, "If you continue seeing that boy, I am going to kill myself." So she broke off the relationship, but she never got over him. Twenty-five years later she found herself in analysis working on her sadness about the end of their love. She reported having dreams of being attacked and raped by gangs of men. Over time, those men became one unknown man. Over more time that one man became this young fellow. That is when she told me the story of her falling in love and her mother's violent reaction.

I said to her, "Well, maybe you should try to find this fellow. It seems to me that there is unfinished business between the two of you and it is attacking you in an emotional way. Whatever is unfinished is harmful to you, and you need to finish it. We need to find out what of your own personality you were or still are projecting onto him and how that is interfering with your own life. Maybe if we understand this we can stop him from being something inside that is thwarting you."

She agreed and went around to her old part of town looking up familiar persons and inquiring about this man. No one had seen or heard from him since high school days. She came back the next hour and said, "Well, I give up."

I said, "Well, we've seen the dreams evolve over time. They will continue evolving, and I have faith that we can work this out on the inside; the dreams will tell us what we need to know. We'll just have to be patient as the dreams slowly show us the meaning of this inner figure." Again she agreed. Then she came back the next week. She walked in my door, white as a ghost, and stammered, "Guess who called . . . from the west coast . . . and simply said, 'Hi, this is J., we have some things to talk about'!" Her response to him, she told me, was a simple, "Yes."

He came to town the next week and they talked about those past years. She realized that she had always admired him for his intelligence and discipline. It was a small step, then, for her to understand how she was seeing in him, in projection, her own mental strengths. The woman was quite intelligent and had a real gift for language. She had never gone to college; her mother did everything she could to keep her creative daughter down. The dreams of being attacked ended when she enrolled at the university.

The next example is from my last months of training in Zürich. I was on the commuter train going to Küsnacht, the suburb where Jung lived and where the C.G. Jung Institute was located. I was sitting in an open train compartment, and a young man was sitting across from me. The rest of the car, which could hold sixty or seventy people, was nearly empty.

It is a custom in Switzerland, even though it is obvious you intend to sit in an empty seat, that before you sit down you say to the people already sitting near, "Is this seat free?" It is more a politeness, a greeting. So this day a person came through and said to us, pointing to seats in our section, "Is this seat free?" The young fellow said, "Actually, I am saving it for a classmate. Would you mind if I keep it for him?" "Fine," the person said agreeably, finding another seating compartment. There were plenty of seats. That happened a second time. When another person came through and asked, "Is this seat free?" The same lad repeated his comment. The reaction from the other person was the same. This happened a third time as someone else came through and the young man made the same request. Remember, this is a nearly empty train car!

There were a couple of older people sitting adjacent to us. They then proceeded to tear into the kid saving the seat: "Who do you think you are, you arrogant little snivel?" "Stop saving that seat." And so on. They were really quite mean, and this made me mad. So I said to them, in my best Swiss German, "Why don't you leave him alone? There are plenty of other seats in the car, he's doing nothing wrong." Well! They then turned their wrath on me.

Noticing my accent, of course, they attacked: "You damn foreigner, we didn't ask you to come here you *scheisskopf* [shithead]; get out of our country, we don't want you here in the first place. Who do you think you are talking to us like this? This isn't your country. We own this train system, not you. Get off this train." Nothing more came of it other than I said some things back to them, accent or no accent, which I will spare you. I let it wash over me, or so I thought.

I was on the train because I was going to an analytic hour. My analyst worked in Küsnacht as well, and then I had to stop by the Jung Institute. So I got off the train and went to my analytic session.

The dream I had had the night before, which I presented for discussion in that hour, was that I was with a woman and she was in bed. She was a very lovely and particularly open-hearted person whom I knew from one of the English classes I was teaching in the Zürich public school system to support myself and pay for my training. In the dream I pulled back the sheet covering her torso and legs and was shocked to find that the inside of her thigh had been gashed from her knee up to her pelvis. There was blood all over the bed, and I awoke.

My analyst said, "Has somebody hurt your feelings?" Women in men's dreams can symbolize feelings and the gash could suggest hurt feelings. I thought for a moment and recalled the scene on the train, "Well, now that you mention it . . . . ," and I told her about what had just happened on the train, although the dream had occurred *before* the event.

We discussed the incident, and she asked, "Why would this be happening now? Why would you have dreamed of hurt feelings and then an event happens which did hurt your feelings?" I said, "After I leave here I'm going to the institute to register for final exams." Then I realized it; I realized that I needed that bad experience to start my summoning up the resolve to leave Switzerland. I had fallen in love with Switzerland and Europe during my studies. I did not want to leave Zürich. But the event made realize that I was not really welcome there. I was a foreigner. I had to leave. I had to leave the grace of living in Europe to get on with my life, or, as my analyst put it, "to go out there and make your mistakes."

First there was the dream, then an event that, so to speak, replayed it. A synchronicity for sure. Then I was left to contemplate its meaning. It was a painful experience but one necessary for me to pluck myself out of Europe and to return to the United States to begin my career as an analyst.

The above examples show how a synchronicity is described by two words: coincidence and meaning. Such events have a purpose. They are not experiences that are "pushed" by the past, but are moments that are trying to pull us into the future. They have an intent that is purposeful, meaningful; in them there is a message concerning our next step in life. Apparently the purpose of a synchronicity is to educate us into a deeper layer of our own genuine self. In order to understand a synchronistic experience we must ask, "What does my psyche want me to do between now and some future time?" The point of view is teleological (from the Greek *telos,* meaning goal). We ask, "What is required of me? What part of me is being encouraged to do what? Where does my life want to go? What is the larger perspective that is trying to develop in my life through this experience? How is this moment a signpost? Synchronistic experiences occur in moments of disorientation and have the effect of providing orientation as they convey the information necessary to bring the future into being.[20]

Consider what an appreciation of synchronicity introduces into our grasp of psychological motivation!

Unquestionably, in Jungian therapy we do know the value of a causal approach. It can be very important to recognize the effect of past events on the way we live. This going back to the past is particularly important when we do not recognize the harm that the past has caused us. An example will illustrate.

---

[20] See also Daryl Sharp, *Jungian Psychology Unplugged: My Life as an Elephant,* p. 7, where the author describes how "chancing" upon a tiny ebony elephant on the Zürich hillside saved him from despair and informed his way forward.

I remember a woman whose father used to pull out a loaded .357 revolver every now and then when she was a child, point it at the members of the family and tell them he was going to kill them—all while shouting invectives. I heard the story several times and finally just erupted: "What a bastard!" She replied, "Oh, no, he was really a very nice man, he just had bad days." That is the kind of denial that calls for more "going back" and re-examining childhood and the emotions that surrounded it. Of course, this woman as an adult kept finding herself in one situation after the other where she was victimized. By her denying the original trauma, it kept repeating. There are many situations where going back and looking at the causes of present behavior has its value. However, not during synchronistic moments!

Just as it is possible to fail to see causes for behavior, so it is possible to fail to see the healing processes of life as they occur in the present. We can easily miss the healing intent of a synchronicity by obsessively turning to past causes—"my uncle's abuse," "my hurt child," for example—so fixated on what happened in the past that we miss the current healing presentiment.

The woman with her experience of the returning friend had been raised, as I noted, by a negative mother, so she looked at life as an awful place that always frustrates. Yet when she experienced life events coming to her aid in a most unlikely fashion, she was touched by an experience in a way that gave her the faith to try again to accomplish something of value for herself. No reductive methodology, no analysis of relationship, no abreaction, no digging into past hurts, no blaming of the mother would have done the same. She was faced with an experience that chopped though her cynicism and, for the first time ever, she felt transported by life. Likewise, in my own situation, I could have talked everlastingly in therapy about why I did not keep my mouth shut in an interchange that had nothing to do with me, or how it is that I can let a stranger hurt my feelings, or what an awful thing xenophobia is. It is not that any of this is untrue; it is that in synchronistic moments such questions are irrelevant. The backward or causative gaze would have missed the real point of the experience.

Both synchronicities came to announce our next challenge in life. We were being invited into a further phase of our development.

## Where are dreams?

The questions that a few moments of reflection lead to after events like I have just described are: Where do dreams occur? In such events, where is the psychological part of ourselves—inside us or outside? We know from the practice of dream analysis that when a dream is understood then the next dream that comes along often picks up the theme of the previous dream and carries it one more step forward.

Dreams, when they are understood, move naturally forward to a more complete understanding of the issue they are dealing with. My analysand and I expected that her dreams would continue dreaming the issue onward, that the psychological issue in her life would continue to be clarified in subsequent dreams, just as they had in the past. Such a development did in fact take place in her life. But it did not occur in dreams "inside" her. It occurred in the form of an outer event that presented her with the same kind of resolution of her suffering that a dream might have offered. At moments like this, *the dream process occurs in the outer world*. That is a mysterious, fascinating fact of synchronicity.

In my own case, experience with dream work makes it clear that I could very well have expected the need to change my attitude toward Switzerland. My need to summon up the resolve to finish my training and leave so many things that I had come to love, would have been taken up by my dreams. The issue approached me, however, not in a dream, but in an event in reality which had the same effect of changing my attitude as a dream normally does. At certain moments, dreams apparently occur not inside us but outside, in events in the outer world. At times, then, outer events may take on the same psychological dynamism, and exhibit the same knowledge in advance of our consciousness, that Jungians have come to take for granted in dreams.

This realization led Jung to say that the psyche, our "inner psychological processes," are not limited to time and space.[21] Dreams and their anticipatory knowledge are not only psychological. The psyche is something much more than that. It is also material.

The two examples illustrate how a synchronistic event can convey knowledge the individual needs to know but does not yet consciously possess. In the bear claw example (page 13), there was no "new" information contained in the synchronicity. It replayed the dream image that the dreamer had just seen. The purpose of the synchronicity was to reinforce the knowledge that she already possessed, to show the dreamer how important this new insight was for the evolving of her life. But in these two most recent examples, the synchronicity conveyed information that neither my analysand nor I were aware of at the time. In both cases synchronicity dreamed the dream forward. The meaningful intervention of the natural world assumed an intelligence in our lives that we ourselves, on our own ability, would not have known.

How can matter operate symbolically, communicating knowledge in advance of our own? How can physical events in time and space act exactly the same way that a dream does? The experience of synchronicity leads us to reevaluate our understanding of the psyche, since obviously it is not only inside us. And it also leads us to reevaluate our understanding of matter. We are led to ask not only, "What is the nature of the psyche?" but also, "What is the nature of matter?" How is matter constructed so that the psyche can impinge on it? What is the connecting link, from the point of view of matter, for the psyche's connection to physical events? Synchronicity challenges our knowledge of both our psychological selves and our grasp of the true nature of the physical world.

Emotionally, the effect of a synchronicity is striking. Once the

---

[21] I use "psyche" to mean the sum of our thoughts, emotions, dreams, etc. In Jung's words: "By psyche I understand the totality of all psychic processes, conscious as well as unconscious." *(Psychological Types*, CW 6, par. 797)

purpose of the synchronistic event is understood, the personal resentment that surrounded it, or the issue from the past that it deals with, evaporates, because we realize that something is happening in the service of a developmental purpose. And when that purpose is understood, the particular pain of a past or present discomforting situation is dissolved. In my analysand's case, when she was moving forward in her life, acquiring the education that gave her the tools to develop her skills and finding a basis for genuine self-worth, the festering of her resentment at being forced to separate from her first love could begin to resolve. And in my case, recognizing the purpose of the event on the train dissolved my resentment at the people whose nastiness was so disagreeable.

This release from hurt is one of the litmus tests of a correct interpretation or understanding of a synchronicity. The recognition of the inner meaning of an outer event has an effect on our emotions that a reductive interpretation could never give. How would it have helped my analysand to understand one more time that her mother's cruelty to her in childhood was keeping her from achieving some goal in the present? She would still have been stuck in self-pity. In my case, investigating the nature of my relation to authority, to the older people sitting across from me, would have yielded no shift in the way I felt about their behavior. Causal interpretation in these instances may satisfy the head, but the heart says, "So what?" We know what may have caused our problem, but ultimately the healing comment comes in the present and looks toward the future.

In both the case of my analysand and myself, our negative emotions were released because, finally, it is addressing life in the present that cleanses and heals a festering wound. Jung never tired of saying this. After the past is explored, additional inquiry into yesterday does not lead to further healing. A change of attitude in the present does, and this change of attitude is exactly the business of a synchronicity. Through it life not only gives us a second chance, it also provides the moral support to move us forward into that chance. The past may have been horrible, but the synchronistic present is a benevolent intervention in life—if we hear and respond.

To sum up: Jung's hypothesis of synchronicity posits that, like the pathway of an electron in an atom, there is a movement to life which is not caused or predicted by past events. In both subatomic and psychological dimensions, motion exhibits a trajectory, and in synchronicity the trajectory is clearly connected with meaning and purpose. The purpose of synchronicity is apparently to direct us toward our life path, to support us when the dark demons of doubt and despair would pull us into false respite. When all of the inner voices say, "You can't," then at times an event in the outer world comes along that has the effect of saying, "You can." A power stronger than our negative voices comes in and the universe says, "Yes." The world acts like an active subject on us, and we, its object, are changed and can move on.

# 2
# Archetypes Are Everywhere

The phenomenon of synchronicity prompted Jung to reevaluate one of his central concepts, that of the archetype. Pauli, meanwhile, realized the challenge that synchronicity and Jung's reflections posed to contemporary science.

Why does synchronicity's portrayal of a dream image in the outer world raise the question of archetypes?

"Archetype" is merely a word that Jung used to indicate that there is something in us creating images. Part of the genius of Jung lay in his ability to make himself very naive and to ask simple questions, such as: "Why is there such a thing as a dream in the first place?"[22] Well, the reason there is a dream in the first place is that there is something in us making them. Jung gave this something a word, and that word is "archetype," which refers to an image-creating factor in the psyche that lies behind our personality and shapes the images we find in our dreams.

Jung first held that the archetype is something psychological, that an image-generating factor within us fashions the emotionally significant images in our dreams. But as he became aware of the phenomenon of synchronicity, he realized there has to be more to it. There must be a dimension of the archetype which is not only psychological, but which is also physical. Otherwise, how could the physical world operate symbolically? How could dream images appear in, or foretell, events in the physical world? Thus Jung realized that the archetype must exist in the physical world as well as in the psyche. This was an extraordinary insight.

Enter Wolfgang Pauli, who in the spirit of a true scientist took synchronicity and its implications very seriously. A PBS

---

[22] "Naiveté is a vice in ordinary life, but in psychology one cannot be naïve enough ... " (Jung, *Visions: Notes of the Seminar*, vol. 1, p. 387).

docmentary called *The Case of ESP* concerning research into the nature of parapsychological phenomena, illustrates the scientific attitude.[23] One vignette in the program presented the work of Dr. Helmut Schmidt,[24] a former research physicist with the Boeing Corporation. Schmidt has documented experiments in which mediums were able to affect the decay rate of uranium by a small but consistent two percent margin. Nineteen scientists working independently, one of them the Dean of the School of Engineering at Princeton University, Dr. Robert Jahn, have consistently been able to duplicate these results. The documentary interviewed scientists antagonistic to these exper-iments and dismissive of their results. Schmidt's reply to the critics is telling. He responded:

> If present physics cannot explain these phenomena, that means that physics isn't complete, and physicists are quite used to drastic changes; they have changed their world-view in the past very often.

Science proceeds by examining the facts that its theories do not explain and generating new theories that encompass the observed phenomena. Synchronicity is one of the facts that science cannot yet explain. Science advances by expanding its theories to elucidate previously unexplained phenomena, not by refuting data it cannot account for. Pauli was interested in how science would develop to be able to recognize and investigate the fact of synchronicity.

Since Pauli was familiar with synchronicity from his own personal experiences as he worked with his dreams, he could not deny that the physical world at times behaves symbolically. He discerned that to incorporate a fuller understanding science must develop beyond its present state to conceive that matter is structured not only by the laws we have seen from physics; at some point what Jung defined as archetype must also be recognized for science to do full justice to the material world which at times acts symbolically.

Science has moved from the magical thinking of the Middle

---

[23] See Tony Edwards, *The Case of ESP.*

[24] Not the same person as the previous chancellor of Germany.

Ages to Newtonian physics and yet again to quantum physics, in intervals of several hundred years; so why would we not expect it to undergo further reevaluation in the future? Pauli, of course, believed that it would. We cannot conceive exactly how that leap will look—just as a medieval alchemist would not have been able to conceive of what the quantum is—because a shift in consciousness is required. Being a creative scientist in the truest sense, Pauli had the breadth of vision to realize that science is a worldview in evolution. After all, had he not been at the center of science's most recent revolution in formulating new laws of matter? It is no wonder, then, that he was willing to continue in the kind of creative scientific thinking that had led to quantum physics in the first place and to continue asking how science may still expand its purview to include synchronicity.

The interests of Jung and Pauli could meet on the nature of the archetype. As Jung realized that the implications of his concept of the archetype needed to be developed in order to accommodate the phenomenon of synchronicity, so Pauli realized that physics' concept of matter must again be modified in order to accommodate the concept of archetype central to synchronicity. Both men saw that the extension of the concept was pertinent to their respective disciplines: Jung because he acknowledged that symbol formation is not limited to our inner psychology and Pauli because he appreciated that science cannot now investigate the meaning of matter as it manifests in synchronicity. Jung knew that, when considered from the point of view of the archetype, the psyche can be material, and Pauli knew, also from the archetypal hypothesis, that matter can be psychological. Jung provided for Pauli the occasion to examine the limits of scientific knowledge. And Pauli provided emotional support for Jung's quest to understand the nature of the "psychological" archetype that can affect, or reflect, physical reality.

This chapter will first examine the development of Jung's hypothesis of the archetype over the course of his life's work. How the phenomenon of synchronicity stimulated Jung to reevaluate this concept and how Pauli played a role in Jung's reassessment will be an essential consideration. Likewise the importance of Jung's point of view for Pauli's professional and personal perspectives will also be discussed.[25]

## C.G Jung and archetypes

We will follow the evolution of Jung's hypothesis of the archetype, as we did with his lifework as a whole, through the four periods identified in the last chapter.

The story of the archetype starts with Jung's discovery of the unconscious and the way it is symbolized in dream images.

As a young resident at the Burghöltzli psychiatric hospital in Zürich, Jung experimented with a word association "test" (Figures 11 and 12, next pages). He would read a patient a list of one hundred words and then ask the person to respond with the first word that came to mind. He informed the patient that he was going to time the replies and record the interval between question and answer. Usually it required a second or two for the patient to come up with a reaction, an "association." The point was not to try to beat the clock, but in a relaxed state to listen to the stimulus word and then to say the first word that came to mind. Though most responses came after a second or two, it took five to ten seconds (or longer) for the patient's response to some of the stimulus words. In general, the patient was able to associate quite easily to some of the stimulus words, but others caused their mental processes to "stumble," so to speak. To some words the subject could not easily come up with an associative reply. By observing this mental process in many of his patients and others, Jung realized that there is something inside all of us that at times can interfere with normal mental processes. Particular words triggered this something inside, preventing the subject of the experiment from associating to these words in the same way that he or she responded to other words.

---

[25] My exposition here necessarily focuses on particular aspects of the archetype. For an authoritative and more comprehensive study, see Anthony Stevens, *Archetype Revisited: A Revised Natural History of the Self.*

| | | | |
|---|---|---|---|
| | 25. go | 51. frog | |
| | 26. blue | 52. try | |
| 1. head | 27. lamp | 53. hunger | 77. cow |
| 2. green | 28. carry | 54. white | 78. name |
| 3. water | 29. bread | 55. child | 79. luck |
| 4. sing | 30. rich | 56. speak | 80. say |
| 5. dead | 31. tree | 57. pencil | 81. table |
| 6. long | 32. jump | 58. sad | 82. naughty |
| 7. ship | 33. pity | 59. plum | 83. brother |
| 8. make | 34. yellow | 60. marry | 84. afraid |
| 9. woman | 35. street | 61. home | 85. love |
| 10. friendly | 36. bury | 62. nasty | 86. chair |
| 11. bake | 37. salt | 63. glass | 87. worry |
| 12. ask | 38. new | 64. fight | 88. kiss |
| 13. cold | 39. habit | 65. wool | 89. bride |
| 14. stalk | 40. pray | 66. big | 90. clean |
| 15. dance | 41. money | 67. carrot | 91. bag |
| 16. village | 42. silly | 68. give | 92. choice |
| 17. pond | 43. book | 69. doctor | 93. bed |
| 18. sick | 44. despise | 70. frosty | 94. pleased |
| 19. pride | 45. finger | 71. flower | 95. happy |
| 20. bring | 46. jolly | 72. beat | 96. shut |
| 21. ink | 47. bird | 73. box | 97. wound |
| 22. angry | 48. walk | 74. old | 98. evil |
| 23. needle | 49. paper | 75. family | 99. door |
| 24. swim | 50. wicked | 76. wait | 100. insult |

Figure 11. List of association experiment stimulus words (1908).

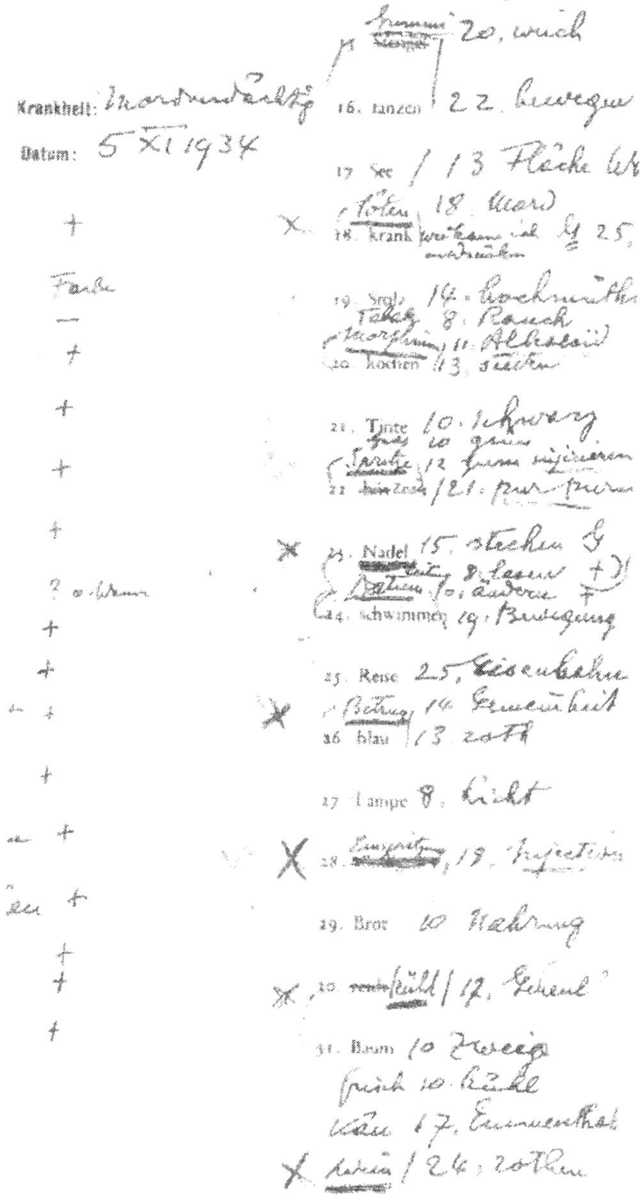

Figure 12. Record of association experiment conducted by Jung.

The results of the word association experiment, as this came to be called, showed that our mental processes can be interrupted by factors beyond our control. The patient was not trying to produce these delays; they just occurred. Further, by discussing both the stimulus and the response words with the subject after the timed part of the process, Jung found that often stories of painful or difficult experiences surfaced. To give some simplistic, hypothetical examples: the stimulus word may have been "green" and the delayed response "heartache." In probing, the patient may have described the end of a love affair in a green room. Or, the stimulus word may have been "ink" and the response "death." The patient may have then come out with a painful experience of having been accused of cheating in school and giving up career dreams. And so on. Jung was struck by the fact that there are "sore spots" in the psyche which become active when something touches on ideas and feelings connected with them, and that this happens quite independently of any intentions of the ego.

Jung also conducted the experiment with patients in his private practice. He even administered it to the public at large, in effect, as he was requested by the courts of Zürich to examine persons on trial. The results were the same: certain words triggered lapses in attention, creating a delay in a person's association, while other words had no such effect. Jung amassed a wealth of data by giving the experiment to a range of individuals: in hospital, and in private and public settings. He published the findings, which formed the basis of one of his fundamental tenets, in "Studies in Word Association."[26] In his observations Jung had come upon the data which led him to posit his concept of the unconscious.

From his work with many subjects, Jung concluded that our psyche is made up of two parts, one conscious and the other unconscious. The former was nothing new but in the world of psychiatry at that time the latter was. Jung first observed this second "system" in us through the way it became active at

---

[26] See *Experimental Researches*, CW 2.

particular moments and disturbed the process of conscious association, and its nature could be ascertained through sensitive questioning concerning the words involved.

We can imagine how excited Jung was to discover Freud's work which also posited the existence of the unconscious. Freud reached his conclusions from observing "forgotten" memories in his patients, memories that seemed largely to circle around painful desires and events in childhood. Jung's research with the association experiment seemed to confirm that these disturbing factors, which exist in hidden parts of the psyche, the "unconscious," had their origin in past childhood experiences. On this basis Freud and Jung could compare their conclusions concerning the nature of this repressed or suppressed part of the psyche and its implications for the process of therapy.

Jung coined the word "complex" to denote the sore spots in the psyche that triggered the delays in associative response; the unconscious, then, was made up of complexes. Complexes are those centers of experience which have been forgotten or, more exactly, stuffed away because they were painful but which are always ready to raise their head when something comes our way that reminds us of the secret pain. A complex then was thought to be a kind of subpersonality that exists in us, a buried organization of experience, thoughts, feelings and reactions which have coalesced from life's painful moments but which can still disrupt our thinking, feeling and behavior when a current experience constellates (activates) the cluster of the painful past.[27]

During this same time period Jung also recognized that these complexes, these centers of potential emotional upset, were symbolized by images in dreams. The emotionally powerful figures in our dreams are pictures of our "subpersonalities," our complexes or painful spots.

---

[27] For a more extensive study of complexes, see Erel Shalit, *The Complex: Path of Transformation from Archetype to Ego.* For briefer comments, see Sharp, *Jungian Psychology Unplugged,* pp. 37ff., and *Digesting Jung: Food for the Journey,* pp. 13ff.:

Still under the influence of the Freudian point of view, Jung wrote his *Psychology of the Unconscious: A Study of the Transformations and Symbolisms of the Libido*, published in 1911 and 1912.[28] The book occasioned his break with Freud, and in it we can already observe Jung beginning to reevaluate his understanding of the complex. Jung's book involved interpreting fantasies and dreams of a young American woman who eventually went through a psychotic episode. In the analysis of her personality, rather than use the word "complex" when describing the effect of the subject's father on her internal psychology, he used the word "imago." And he explains in a footnote:

> Here I purposely give preference to the term "imago" rather than to "complex," in order to make clear, by this choice of a technical term, that the psychological factor which I sum up under "imago" has a living independence in the psychic hierarchy, i.e., possesses that *autonomy* which wide experience has shown to be the essential feature of feeling-toned complexes.[29]

The shift is subtle but perceptible. By giving preference to "imago" Jung became more interested in how the complex manifests itself to us as an image than in where in our past experience it arises. In other words, his focus began to shift from how the complex is caused to how it is pictured as an inner reality on its own terms. He was becoming attentive to how the complex could turn into an image or symbol.[30] He was concerned less with the factors causing the complex and more with those influencing its representation in dreams and fantasies. Even the word "image" would not do. He did not want to convey something static, but something dynamic, so he took the word "imago" from Latin to divest it of any idea of stasis.

---

[28] The original German title (*Wandlungen und Symbole der Libido*) might be more accurately translated as simply *Transformations and Symbols of the Libido*. The book was rewritten in 1952 and published as *Symbols of Transformation*, CW 5.

[29] *Symbols of Tansformation,* CW 5, par. 62, n. 4.

[30] See Liliane Frey-Rohn, *From Freud to Jung,* p. 167.

Of course, even in its first formulation, the complex was understood as a dynamic presence in the unconscious, since it could interrupt mental processes in the way that the association experiment evidenced. But, in that first conceptualization, the complex was something whose existence was *dependent* on its cause, as we have seen. Jung, in the above passage, however, clearly stressed the living independence of this inner reality, initially conceived as a product of past hurts. The term imago emphasized the idea that these inner complexes can have a living and independent existence in ourselves, often with an intent of their own.

By choosing the word imago, Jung indicated that his concern was going to be the portrait of these inner parts of the psyche, how they appeared, how they acted inside a person, what their characteristics were as they showed up in dreams and behavior. Whereas the initial recognition of their existence in our psyche underscored their negative effects, as seen in the association experiment, Jung soon grasped that this was a far too limited portrayal of their role. Surely some of them have this negative effect, interrupting our intentions and working against us, but not all of them do and not all of the time. By shifting to the word imago, Jung was refining his notion of these inner psychological subpersonalities. They may be rooted in past pain and deleterious to happy living, but they can also be sources of creativity and emotional largesse. Rather than being negative, they can actually contribute to the fullness of creative production and emotionally rich living. They can be a product but they can also be a source of living, dynamic independence.

In the first phase of Jung's life (1875 to 1913), he established the existence of the unconscious and its complexes, extending his focal point from the cause of complexes to their symbolization. The next step in Jung's defining and redefining the archetype came in the second period of his life, during his night sea journey (1913 to 1928).

During this period he further developed the idea that he had first given expression to in the word imago. In 1919 he used the term "archetype" for the first time:[31]

> Just as the instincts compel us to a specifically human mode of existence, so archetypes force our ways of perception and apprehension into specifically human patterns.[32]

Jung had distinguished that there are factors within the psyche shaping the images that we see in our dreams. It next became increasingly clear how these inner parts, and the images that symbolized them, were not merely a product of experience. Another inner factor contributed to the form of the images we perceive in our night stories. Personal experience may play a role in their formation, but there is an inner dynamic, the archetype, that is also involved in shaping their final form. That final form was what resided, so to speak, in the unconscious and exerted influence on our thinking, feeling and behavior.

Jung continues:

> Archetypes are typical modes of apprehension, and wherever we meet with uniform and regularly recurring modes of apprehension we are dealing with an archetype.[33]

We all come with built-in "modes of apprehension," structural dispositions to perceive and conceive. They also have an effect on our lives as they shape the unconscious contents within us. These predispositions are part of our instinctual heritage.

What are instincts? At the Wildfowl Trust in England many rare waterfowl are hatched and reared by Bantam hens to increase their chances of survival in captivity. Baby ducks and swans thus raised still swim naturally. Likewise at maturity these birds will mate with

---

[31] See "Instinct and the Unconscious," *The Structure and Dynamics of the Psyche*, CW 8, par. 270, n.7. See also Frey-Rohn, *From Freud to Jung*, p. 92. For a time during this period Jung also used the term "primordial image" instead of the word archetype, but eventually the words primordial image were dropped.

[32] "Instinct and the Unconscious," *The Structure and Dynamics of the Psyche*, CW 8, par. 270.

[33] Ibid., par. 280.

their own species, exhibiting the normal behaviors and conventions of courtship of their type despite their previously never having seen one of their own kind. Clearly early experience and learning is not the only determinant of the animals' behavior.[34] Swimming and mating are instinctual behaviors. This is in complete agreement with Jung:

> Instincts are typical modes of action, and wherever we meet with uniform and regularly recurring modes of action and reaction we are dealing with instinct.[35]

An instinct is an inherited behavior pattern, such as the above swimming and mating. Jung categorized five main human instincts: sexuality, activity, hunger, reflection and creativity.[36] Just as there are typical instincts, so there are typical predispositions for experience and understanding. To put it at its most basic, when we are motivated by our instincts, we are not merely living and behaving in an instinctual way, we are also perceiving our actions within that instinctual process. Just as the sex instinct or the aggression instinct lead to typical behaviors, we also have feelings, thoughts and fantasies as we behave instinctually in those ways. The archetype is the inborn factor that shapes the experience of our instinctual behavior. What the instinct is to behavior, the archetype is to experience, hence Jung called the archetype the "self-portrait of the instinct."[37]

So our instinctual inheritance and the predispositions toward experience which accompany it are important aspects of our unconscious with its "nodes" of influence on behavior. In the second part of Jung's life he added the archetypal factor with its instinctual roots to his understanding of what makes us tick. Not everything in us is there by virtue of its being a simple imprint of

---

[34] See Ellen P. Reese and P.P.G. Bateson, *Imprinting*.

[35] "Instinct and the Unconscious," *The Structure and Dynamics of the Psyche*, CW 8, par. 273.

[36] "Psychological Factors in Human Behavior," ibid., par. 246.

[37] "Instinct and the Unconscious," ibid., par. 277.

our individual experience. The presence of images in our dreams—and the parts of ourselves which these images symbolize—are not profitably understood in the end by diving into our past, important as this may be at times. Thus it was to those images—the way they appeared and behaved in dreams—that Jung turned more and more in this second part of his life, not necessarily concentrating on their cause because the images were also shaped by archetypal factors from within. Our images show us who we are; what the images refer to may have a genesis in the past, but the images themselves have been formed and shaped by inner archetypal patterns. So why not just take them as they appear? Jung became more interested in the characteristics and behavior of our inner images than he was in where they came from. This first recognition of the archetype, its effect on our inner images and our personality, was another fruit of Jung's dark days after his separation from Freud.

In the third period of his life (1928 to 1944), Jung continued refining his understanding of the archetype and how it functioned to shape the inner psychological material that we see personified in our dreams and fantasies. The archetype's power to exert a strong influence on psychological experience, and hence behavior, continued to attract his attention. Jung wrote in 1940, during his "nuts and bolts" period:

> Archetypes are . . . factors and motifs that arrange the psychic elements into certain images, characterized as archetypal, but in such a way that they can be recognized only from the effects they produce.[38]

---

[38] "A Psychological Approach to the Dogma of the Trinity," *Psychology and Religion*, CW 11, par. 222, n. 2. For example, in the earlier story of the bear claw, bears were something the dreamer of course knew from personal experience, but the dream "used" or "arranged" the bear image to refer to a psychological issue related to the maternal aspect of the dreamer's personality. This is in accord with the fact that bears are indeed known to be a mother representation throughout myth and fairy tales. Thus the presence of the bear image in the woman's life was shaped by an archetypal factor, not merely by her personal knowledge of bears.

Or, in this same time period, he called the archetype a formative principle of the "image-creating mind."[39] The archetypes became centers of creative and healing impact. The emphasis was continually toward the regulating and healing activity of the archetype on what is going on inside us. Developing this idea Jung wrote:

> The archetype determines the nature of the configurational process and the course it will follow, with seeming foreknowledge, or as though it were already in possession of the goal to be circumscribed by the centring process.[40]

Jung recognized that once images were accepted in the analytic process they began to transform. They reflected a coherent development toward a goal, an intelligence, a foreknowledge, of how our lives can most meaningfully develop—a knowledge often far greater than what the conscious mind can muster. What a difference from the original view of the unconscious that Jung first formulated as a young psychiatrist and that had drawn him into association with Freud! For Jung, the agency of the past is increasingly seen against the creative power of the psyche; when it seizes on our psychological material and begins to transform it, this creative power is as potent a factor in shaping our personality as is past experience. Thus the unconscious is no longer a nuisance but a source of positive stimulus and direction; its images have an inherent capacity to grow forward if we can understand and respond to them, ever leading us into a personally authentic future. Recall how the woman's dreams of her past boyfriend evolved over time to tell her what she needed to know about the direction her life could take; the teenage experience of the boy became a living image in her in its own right, changing as awareness of herself developed in analysis.

---

[39] "Psychological Commentary on the *Tibetan Book of the Great Liberation*," *Psychology and Religion*, CW 11, par. 781.

[40] "On the Nature of the Psyche," *The Structure and Dynamics of the Psyche*, CW 8, par. 411.

Who we are is not only the product of what we have been but also the result of the transmuting power of the archetype which can metamorphose unconscious parts of ourselves into new forms. Possessing foreknowledge, archetypal images can provide a path toward their (hence, our) future developments which we could not have invented consciously. Thus, in the second phase of his life Jung posited the archetype as an image-creating and image-shaping factor within the psyche; and in this third phase he more fully examined its efficacy as an independent, creative and intelligent factor capable of healing purpose, an organizing, ordering and transformative principle in its own right.

Of the fourth period of Jung's life (1944 to 1961), Liliane Frey-Rohn, another trusted analyst-interpreter of Jung's work, notes:

> In his works during his last years Jung's view of the world deepened to such an extent that it not only transcended its earlier framework but put it in a wholly new perspective. He ventured into areas so little known to medical psychology that it is hardly possible to see Jung's mature concepts in the same context as those Freud had voiced earlier.[41]

This fundamental shift centers on Jung's recognition of the extent to which his synchronicity hypothesis forced a reconsideration of much of what he had already written. Synchronicity showed that the material world is not only something inert and out there, the presupposition that had previously been hidden within Jung's thinking. Wider categories of understanding are necessary to explain events in the outer world and the full range of human nature that synchronicity uncovers.

Pauli played a great role in helping Jung find confidence in what he said during the last years of his life. Jung obviously knew that his writings contradicted science in the narrow sense, and he repeatedly voiced the pain of being marginalized by established thinkers.[42] Pauli, much to his credit and no doubt thanks to the dark

---

[41] Frey-Rohn, *From Freud to Jung*, p. 281.

[42] Jung to Pauli: "If you feel isolated from your contemporaries when grappling

nights he himself had experienced, was emotionally convinced of the reality of synchronistic phenomena. For Jung to have Pauli, a Nobel laureate in physics, express interest in his work, and encourage its publication, meant a great deal. As he wrote to Pauli: "I am particularly indebted to you for having given me new heart."[43]

Jung's reflections at this point pertain to the earlier question, "Where do dreams occur?" We have seen that the archetypal hypothesis was formed to explain *psychological* phenomena. There is an archetypal factor that actively shapes psychological elements into the recognizable images we find in our dreams and fantasies. The archetype is not too hard to imagine when we link it to the instinct, as the mental side of the instinct. As stated, what the instinct is to action the archetype is to experience, a potentiality for certain types of experience and for their power to work on us. But, if matter can act symbolically, where is the archetype? Clearly the definition of the archetype is not exhausted with a merely psychological consideration. The archetype must also impinge on matter, insofar as matter functions symbolically.

Jung coined the word "psychoid" to express this dimension of the archetype:

It seems to me probable that the real nature of the archetype is not capable of being made conscious, that it is transcendent, on which account I call it psychoid.[44].

In my previous writings I have always treated archetypal phenomena as psychic, because the material to be expounded or investigated was concerned solely with ideas and images. The psychoid nature of the archetype . . . does not contradict these earlier formations; it only

---

with the unconscious, it is also the same with me, in fact more so, since I am actually standing in the isolated area, striving somehow to bridge the gap that separates me from the others. After all, it is no pleasure for me always to be regarded as esoteric." (Meier, ed., *Atom and Archetype*, p. 129)

[43] Ibid., p. 68.

[44] "On the Nature of the Psyche," *The Structure and Dynamics of the Psyche*, CW 8, par. 417.

means a further degree of conceptual differentiation, which became inevitable as soon as I saw myself obliged to undertake a more general analysis of the nature of the psyche and to clarify the empirical concepts concerning it and their relation to one another.[45]

The "more general analysis" was, of course, instigated by Jung's reflections on the nature of synchronicity and the challenge it poses to recognize the archetype as an experience- and image-shaping factor that belongs to the objective world as well. Jung continues:

> In archetypal conceptions and instinctual perceptions, spirit and matter confront one another on the psychic plane. Matter and spirit both appear in the psychic realm as distinctive qualities of conscious contents.[46]

Matter and spirit, outer world and inner, are the two places where the archetype touches us. What we had thought was "psychological" is merely one pole of the archetype, its nature extending between our inner world and the outer world. Clearly the archetype is not just a psychological concept, it also extends to the material world in a way which we do not fully understand. But we can recognize and describe it. Jung writes:

> Since psyche and matter are contained in one and the same world, and moreover are in continuous contact with one another and ultimately rest on irrepresentable, transcendental factors, it is not only possible but fairly probable, even, that psyche and matter are two different aspects of one and the same thing. The synchronicity phenomena point, it seems to me, in this direction, for they show that the nonpsychic can behave like the psychic, and vice versa, without there being any causal connection between them. Our present knowledge does not allow us to do much more than compare the relation of the psychic to the material world with two cones, whose apices, meeting in a point without extension—a real zero point—touch and do not touch.[47]

---

[45] Ibid., par. 419.

[46] Ibid., par. 420.

[47] Ibid., par. 418.

Apparently the psyche has roots in the material realm, and in the background of the psyche are to be found nonpsychic factors of consequence which through matter can communicate to us knowledge of who we are.

The archetype as something more than psychological, that is, psychoid, brings us back to Wolfgang Pauli. We have seen that he was very supportive of Jung's efforts to understand synchronicity and the complications it introduces into our world-view. In fact, Jung credited Pauli for the suggestion to begin publishing on synchronicity in the first place. He wrote to Pauli in 1949:

> Quite a while ago, you encouraged me to write down my thoughts on synchronicity. I have finally managed to get around to it and more or less collect my thoughts on the subject.[48]

And an editorial note in the Pauli-Jung letters tells us that several versions of this essay were given to Pauli for comment and each time the corrections Pauli made were incorporated until the final essay was finished:

> The manuscripts for Jung's evolving "Synchronicity" essay are at the ETH Library, Zürich . . . . As changes occurred as a result of Jung's discussions with Pauli, one can compare points of discussion in the letters with the published [German] version of 1952.[49]

Pauli, supportive of Jung's work, was in turn touched by Jung's inquiry. The role of matter in symbols induced Jung to ask with Pauli's help, "What is the archetype?" The role of symbols in matter would similarly induce Pauli to ask, with Jung's help, "What is matter?"

## Wolfgang Pauli and matter

Our discussion now turns to Pauli's appreciation for Jung's archetypal hypothesis, particularly his notion of the psychoid arche-

---

[48] Meier, ed., *Atom and Archetype*, p. 36.

[49] Ibid., p. 38, note; The full title of Jung's essay is "Synchronicity: An Acausal Connecting Principle," *The Structure and Dynamics of the Psyche*, CW 8.

type and its relation to matter. Jung's view was pertinent to Pauli's work as a physicist in two respects: first, in its corroboration of the "just so" quality in the numerical structure of matter and the configuration of the electrons' orbits, and second, in helping him conceptualize the nature of the creative imagination in science.

After looking at Pauli's conscious views concerning the importance of the archetype for physics' research into matter, in the next chapter I will explore the reaction of Pauli's unconscious to these same ideas. Pauli thoughtfully left a record of his dreams concerning the evolution of his appreciation of synchronicity and its bearing on the archetype. A dream figure, which he called the "Stranger," representing just this principle of nature that contemporary science cannot quantify, is prevalent in Pauli's unconscious imagery and he gave ongoing attention to it. Also, Pauli's dream shortly after a key discussion with Jung on these matters is available to us and is taken up in the next chapter. The unconscious side of Pauli's outlook, and its personal meaning for him, will occupy us shortly.

But first we will look at some of Pauli's reflections concerning archetypes, science and matter.

Planck's constant and its whole number multiples which quantify the electrons' orbital levels in the atom struck Pauli very forcibly. This intrinsic patterning has always puzzled physicists. Another example of this puzzling regularity in matter is the decay rates of radioactive elements such as uranium. A hunk of uranium decays at an utterly predictable rate; the average decay rate of all the atoms in the hunk does not vary. But how the average rate can be so precise, when very few individual atoms in that hunk actually conform to the average, remains an enigma to scientists.

From examining the "just so" regularity of matter, Pauli surmised that there must be some organizing principle within it. Jung's psychoid archetype provided the bridge here, and Pauli could easily see its relevance to grasping the nature of matter's just-so structures. Just as the archetype is the factor behind the creation of dreams and the link between the dream and matter, so it might also be an organizing principle in matter itself. For Pauli, as a physicist, the psychoid archetype became not only a hypothesis concerning the nature of the psyche and its connection to the physical world, but also a possible way to visualize an organizing principle central to the makeup of matter. The archetype was for Pauli an ordering principle which is "neutral in respect of the distinction psychical-physical."[50] From their dialogue, Pauli and Jung developed the idea of the psychoid archetype and thought it relevant to unraveling the orderedness of matter per se. Pauli felt that additional research in physics might, in time, involve the further understanding or evolution of the concept of the psychoid archetype in psychology,[51] and that similarly the recognition of (psychoid) archetypal patterns within matter might contribute further to our understanding of the material world:

> In physics . . . we do not speak of . . . "archetypes," but of "statistical laws of nature involving primary possibilities"; but both formulations meet in their tendency to extend the old narrower idea of "causality" (determinism) to a more general form of connections in nature, a conclusion to which the psycho-physical problem also points.[52]

The laws of nature with "just so" quantities as their primary foundation—and the archetype's ordering effect on images in the psyche—both show a "more general form of connections." Thus the research of one discipline may contribute in time to the research of the other, and hence our knowledge of both psychological and physical processes might advance conjointly.

Already in the above formulation Pauli had widened the concept of archetype in a very interesting fashion that allowed it to apply to matter as well as to the psyche. Whereas Jung presented his concept of the archetype essentially as the inborn capacity to pattern experience, Pauli introduced the notion of probability into this definition. Jung wrote to Pauli:

---

[50] "Ideas of the Unconscious," in Pauli, *Writings on Physics and Philosophy*, p. 159.

[51] Ibid., p. 164.

[52] Ibid.; see also Meier, ed., *Atom and Archetype*, p. 64.

> Your idea that the probability concept in mathematics corresponds to the archetype was most illuminating. In fact, the archetype represents nothing else but the probability of psychic events. . . . This can probably be best seen in the tendency of the archetype to keep reproducing and confirming itself . . . [by creating archetypal images].
>
> Under these circumstances, you are fully justified in demanding a new interpretation of the term archetype.[53]

The small addition of the word "probability" to Jung's formulation of the archetypal concept makes a noteworthy difference. With that twist, the archetype as applicable to the formation of images in dreams and fantasies and the archetype as germane to matter converge in statistical likelihood. In both cases the archetype can be acknowledged as a probability: the probability that life will be experienced in a particular fashion recognized from past precedent as "archetypal," and the probability that subatomic movement will occur over a range of alternative possibilities.

Just as there are probabilities associated with the path of the electron in an excited atom, so the archetype represents a tendency to produce and shape images of a specific character in specific instinctual or emotionally laden moments of life. It is still unclear how embellishing the archetype concept will further research, and whether it will bear fruit first in psychology or first in physics. Both Pauli and Jung were well aware that their work raised as many questions as it answered. They were simply trying to see things in a new fashion and to reexamine an old split in any way that could lead to further inquiry. It is not the first time that we will hear, and spoken without apology, "I feel as though I am groping my way through dense fog."[54]

Another area where Pauli found Jung's sense of the psychoid archetype relevant for the work of a physicist was in understanding the nature of the creative processes within the scientist. How is it

---

[53] Ibid., pp. 69f.

[54] Jung to Pauli, in ibid., p. 68.

that we can know the laws of the universe and its matter at all? Pauli found the concept of the psychoid archetype to be an essential contribution to that age-old query. He surmised from the notion of the psychoid that the forms of matter are also the forms of the psyche, that the archetype exists in both matter and the psyche, and through the identity of the two forms matter is known. He wrote:

> What is the nature of the bridge between the sense perceptions and the concepts? All logical thinkers have arrived at the conclusion that pure logic is fundamentally incapable of constructing such a link.[55]

And:

> The conscious realization of new knowledge seems thus to be based on a correspondence, a "matching" of inner images pre-existent in the human psyche with external objects and their behavior.[56]

The reason we can know anything about the inner workings of the material world is that there is a coincidence between our own thought-forms and the processes going on in matter. "To know" means to link up the inner archetypal patterns of the psyche with those that structure the outer world. And "knowing" first happens in images and emotions before it becomes thoughts and concepts. Considering the process by which scientific theories originate, Pauli expressed the view that

> all understanding is a long-drawn-out process initiated by processes in the unconscious long before the content of consciousness can be rationally formulated ... . On this level the place of clear concepts is taken by images with strong emotional content, not thought out but beheld. . . . . As a consequence of the rationalistic attitude of scientists since the eighteenth century, the background processes that accompany the development of the natural sciences, although present as always and of decisive effect, remained to a large extent unheeded.[57]

---

[55] "The Influence of Archetypal Ideas on the Scientific Theories of Kepler," in Pauli, *Writings on Physics and Philosophy*, p. 220.

[56] Ibid., p. 221.

[57] Ibid.

By examining the origin and development of concepts and theories in natural science, Pauli suggested that there was a relationship between inner archetypal ideas and scientific theories of the outer world.[58]

An example will illustrate Pauli's point. The structure of the benzene ring, a six-sided polygon, came to its discoverer, August Kekulé, in 1865 in a dream. The benzene ring is a common structure in organic matter and consists of six carbon atoms hooked together in a sort of six-sided circle or hexagon (Figure 13). I quote from Kekulé's own description in an 1890 speech to the German Chemical Society in honor of the twenty-fifth anniversary of his discovery of the formula. He first discussed how dreams had contributed to previous insights, and then continued:

> During my stay in Ghent (1865) I lived in fashionable bachelor quarters in the High Street. But my study was in a narrow side street and during the daytime it had no light. For a chemist, who spends his daylight hours in the laboratory, this was not really a disadvantage. I simply sat there and wrote away at my textbook. And yet somehow I couldn't get it going properly. My mind was on other things. I turned my chair to the fire and *dozed*. Again the atoms were gamboling before my eyes. This time the smaller groups kept modestly in the background. My mental eye, rendered more acute by repeated visions of this kind, could now distinguish larger structures, of manifold conformation, long rows, all twining and twisting in snakelike motion. But look! What was that? One of the snakes had seized hold of its own tail, and the form whirled mockingly before my eyes. As if by a flash of lightening I awoke. This time, too, I spent the rest of the night working out the implications of the hypothesis.
>
> Let us learn to dream, gentlemen; then, perhaps, we shall discover the truth.[59]

---

[58] Ibid., p. 222.

[59] Meier, *The Unconscious in Its Empirical Manifestations*, pp. 19ff.

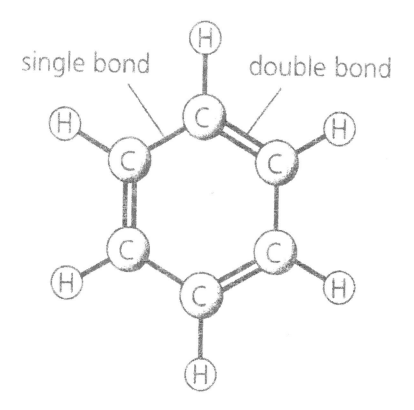

Figure 13.The benzene ring.

C.A. Meier's commentary on this dream is worthy of note:

The Greek alchemists called this snake Ouroborus . . the tail-eater [figure 14], and very often made it their central symbol. . . .The ancient interpretation of the Ouroborus [is] a symbol that unites the opposites. . . .

It is undoubtedly an archetypal image in the sense in which Jung used that term.[60]

Figure 14. The Ouroboros

---

[60] Ibid., pp. 22f.

Such a symmetrical and circular figure is a well-known archetypal image in dreams and one of the central, recurring symbols representing the structure of the psyche—the mandala.[61]

In the case of Kekulé we can clearly see the relation between an archetypal image and the form in which matter is constructed, an example of the psychoid dimension of the archetype that Pauli felt could be constructively applied to our understanding of how scientific creativity works—in the way both outer matter and inner psychology overlap. The archetype pertains to both psyche and matter and is what allows the former to see into the structure of the latter. Thus, Pauli was keenly interested in the influence of archetypal images on the developments of science.

In conclusion, the hypothesis of the psychoid archetype spoke to both Jung and Pauli with respect to the parallel structures of matter and psyche. Both saw that continued research in their respective fields might shed light on the psychoid archetype.

How did all of this affect Pauli personally? To show how Pauli's own life was emotionally touched by this dialogue between matter and spirit I will now turn to several of his dreams which occurred during the time that he and Jung passionately discussed their mutual concerns.

---

[61] I will be talking more about mandalas in chapter 4.

# 3
# The Stranger Knows

The inner figure that Pauli called the "Stranger" first appeared in his dreams shortly after he and Jung had an important discussion concerning the nature of synchronicity.[62] We will observe that the Stranger represents the unity of spirit and matter posited by Jung's formulation of the psychoid archetype. By Pauli's own account, this new image was a synthesis of two other similar figures that previously appeared in his dreams.[63] Although the new image shared some characteristics with the previous two, it was also different in some ways. This chapter will trace the development of the Stranger in Pauli's inner life by initially examining the two earlier figures in two separate dreams so that we can see the characteristics of each; then I will provide an account of the dream in which the two figures were united in the Stranger image shortly after Pauli's meeting with Jung; and finally I will examine what this inner Stranger image was asking of Pauli.

Whereas in the previous chapter we tried to understand the link between spirit and matter in a theoretical way, here that link is personified by Pauli's unconscious as a dream image rich in meaning. The unconscious, with its facility to symbolize psychological reality, has provided us with an image of the very phenomenon we are trying to understand. By investigating that image we are exploring another venue for appreciating the link between spirit and matter.

---

[62] This chapter and the next rely on two main sources: Meier, ed., *Atom and Archetype* and Herbert van Erkelens, *Wolfgang Pauli und der Geist der Materie*. Van Erkelens diligently searched archives and publications to collect Pauli's extant dreams. I have not referenced van Erkelens' commentary on the dreams where it followed an expected line of inquiry. Those points where his analysis presents a novel thread have been noted. His solid work is clearly a labor of love, and it is much appreciated.

[63] Meier, ed., *Atom and Archetype*, pp. 30, 43.

When we apply our tools of symbolic interpretation to Pauli's dream image of the Stranger, we avail ourselves of an imaginative perspective on the symmetry between spirit and matter, inner and outer, subject and object, psyche and world. Previously we looked at thought formulations of the psychoid archetype; here we will look at image formulations. Images from Pauli's unconscious will assist us in our inquiry to comprehend the psychoid archetype and its emotional meaning for personal experience.

**The blond man**

In a letter to Jung dated October 23, 1946, Pauli included the following dream:

> Through the post I receive a small chest. Inside it is apparatus for the experimental investigation of cosmic rays. Next to it is a tall, blond man. He seems to be somewhat younger than me (maybe between 30 and 40). He says: "You must force the water up higher than the houses in the city so that the city dwellers will believe you." Then behind the apparatus in the little box I notice a bunch of *keys*, 8 in all, arranged in a circle with the key-bits hanging down.[64]

In his commentary to the dream Pauli wrote:

> The water and the city are allusions to earlier dreams. In these dreams there was a dark, male figure playing a role who appeared as a "Persian" who had not been accepted as a student at the Institute of Technology (contrast to the prevailing scientific collective opinion). "The Blond" and "The Persian" may be dual aspects of one and the same figure (they never appear together). The figure has an extremely "psychopompos" character and has a similar function to Mercury with the alchemists. . . . It was only in June of the following year that I dreamed that the water had drained off.[65]

There is no record of the earlier dreams Pauli referred to in his commentary.[66] But the motif of flooding is a common one in

---

[64] Ibid.; see also van Erkelens, *Wolfgang Pauli*, p. 37 (dream 2).

[65] Meier, ed., *Atom and Archetype*, p. 30.

[66] Van Erkelens, *Wolfgang Pauli*, p. 37.

dreams, and it is usually interpreted as depicting an inundation from the unconscious. When we are overcome with moods or depression and feel ourselves overwhelmed, it is very likely that we will dream of floods or of being in danger of drowning. So it is very probable that the flooding theme here refers to Pauli's sense of being overcome. We know that he was prone to dark moods, some that even incapacitated him and forced him to his bed.[67] While it is possible that this dream refers to a transitory mood triumphing over Pauli, he tells us in his remarks that it took a year for the water to subside in a subsequent dream. Thus the flooding probably alludes to more than just a transitory state of mind, but rather to a state of mind bigger than a day- or week-long mood. Likely, it suggests an ongoing emotional disturbance.

Pauli's description of feeling depressed and disillusioned concerning the role that physics played in producing atomic weapons is suggestive:

As in Austria during the First World War, in the year [1945] while I stayed in America I suddenly had the distinct feeling that I lived in a criminal atmosphere. That was at the time when the atomic bombs had been dropped on Japan. . . . My anima got very irritated and had outbursts of anger till I departed from the USA (in February 1946).[68]

I feel myself relatively well to be back in Switzerland, where at least the people and the country are not involved in this kind of collective

---

[67] Ibid., pp. 64, 100.

[68] Karl von Meyenn, ed., *Wolgang Pauli. Wissenschaftlicher Briefwechel mit Bohr, Einstein, Heisenberg u.a.* [hereafter *Briefwechsel*] *Band IV/Teil I,1950 – 1952*, p. 306 (cited in van Erkelens, *Wolfgang Pauli*, p. 35). Anima is the name Jung gave to the feminine part of a man's personality, the "inner woman." She is accordingly symbolized in a man's dreams by female figures. She generally personifies the man's moods, emotions and feelings, as well as his capacity for rapport in relationship. She is a determining figure in the man's unconscious cast of characters since she is closely tied with eros and sexual attraction. As Pauli was finding out, she also has a very definite point of view, and puts challenges to men to integrate her way of looking at life by creating all sorts of emotional storms until he shuts up and starts listening to her perspective

guilt (neither in the First World War nor the use of the atom bomb in 1945). . . . Yet now something perhaps worse has arisen: indeed my (geographical) surroundings are *not* mired in guilt, but certainly my profession, *physics*, is.

My consciousness attitude is that it is unreasonable to give up physics because of these political and military experiences: science is not responsible for the uses to which it is put by others—indeed these uses can always be to the useful or the harmful. But the unconscious, the anima, holds a different view. It seems she is, in this regard, developing resistances against physics and will see to it that I cease having creative ideas, or at least fewer of them. Will the new experience in 1945 prompt me towards a spiritual development that leads away from physics in the narrower sense? Perhaps such a step has already been constellated. .. I know it is a question of fate that, in the end, is something beyond my decision.[69]

This sounds more like the kind of flood that the dream is talking about. Pauli was inundated by doubts and discouraging emotions about physics and its role in his time. Even though he could rationally tell himself on the conscious level that it was silly to hold physics responsible for the atomic end of World War Two, his unconscious felt otherwise and plagued him with a malaise strong enough to interfere with his ability to work. No matter what he thought consciously, he anticipated his creativity in science could dry up in his despair, and such an effect from the unconscious shows that it had its own point of view which could overcome and paralyze his waking life. His upset with physics was an inundation of an unconscious standpoint that held a different point of view than his conscious one. This is probably what the flood was about.

Pauli's recognition of his unconscious standpoint, indicated in the above quote, is a beautiful example of what it means for a man to take account of his inner world and the figures of the unconscious he finds there. In Pauli's case this figure is the anima—since his moods were affected. Attending to the anima is not a matter of merely simmering chicken soup or baking biscuits

---

[69] Von Meyenn, ed., *Briefwechsel*, p. 307; van Erkelens, *Wolfgang Pauli*, pp. 35f.

for the soul as we may have heard from pop psychology, but of listening inside and recognizing that there is a fundamentally different point of view in the unconscious. Coming to terms with that other point of view in the unconscious—in Pauli's case the anima, his inner woman—means integratng new attitudes toward life.

The flood in Pauli's dream signifies the challenge to experience and digest the other standpoint and to modify his conscious point of view accordingly. In the final analysis Pauli was being flooded with another way of looking at his present historical time and at what changes needed to be incorporated into its dominant attitudes. The challenge to do this attacked him in the form of emotional outbursts, guilt and a fear of creative lethargy, but underneath those states of mind a definite and specific challenge to his conscious standpoint was taking place.

Pauli extends this very same idea when he writes:

> The "cosmic rays" in the dreams are not the real cosmic rays of physics. They are actually suprapersonal (archetypal) contents but not yet made more specific.[70]

Accordingly, the dream is suggesting to Pauli the necessity of accepting his distress and malaise as a signal that it is time to begin investigating the other point of view, represented also by the "suprapersonal (archetypal) contents," that have yet to be "made more specific." These contents were another representation of what was pressuring Pauli through his mood of despair.

The flood waters in the dream were being driven up even higher, so the mood would continue to intensify and upset Pauli emotionally. As Pauli was to find a new world-view, the "city dwellers," the conventional citizen in Pauli, had to be discombobulated with a rising emotional flood to loosen his confidence in his previous way of looking at life and science.

All of this comes at the hands of the Blond. Pauli's comments in a letter to Emma Jung are instructive:

---

[70] Meier, ed., *Atom and Archetype*, p. 210, Appendix 7.

Everything that Prof. Jung says about the "spirit Mercurius" fits him perfectly. . . . My dream figure is also "dual-layered"; on the one hand, he is a spiritual-light figure with superior knowledge, and on the other hand, he is a chthonic natural spirit. . . . He is the one who prepares the way for the quaternity, which is always pursuing him. He regards everyone around him (especially me) as completely ignorant and uneducated compared with himself. He does not reject the ancient writings on magic but simply regards them as a popular preliminary stage for people with no education (e.g., myself). He is not an Antichrist, but in a certain sense an "Antiscientist," "science" here meaning especially the scientific approach, particularly as it is taught in universities today.[71] This he sees as a sort of *Zwinguri*,[72] as the place and symbol of his oppression, which (in my dreams) he occasionally sets fire to.[73] . . . This "stranger" is something that did not accept the scientific world picture about 300 years ago and is now running around autonomously in the collective unconscious like a loose canon . . . . When rational methods in science reach a dead end, a new lease of life is given to those contents that were pushed out of time cnsciousness in the 17th century and sank into the unconscious.[74]

In his own words, Pauli is introducing us to the dream figure of the Stranger. The blond man who instigates the flood represents one half of the Stranger, the "spiritual-light" side of this figure with "superior knowledge." So the flood theme also indicates that the new way of comprehending, introduced to Pauli through his emotional suffering, is the standpoint of the blond man.[75] The blond man signifies the "light" or "mental" or "understanding" aspect of the new point of view which will later be incorporated into the fuller figure of the Stranger. Pauli was being pressured to think

---

[71] Exemplified in the reactions given to Helmut Schmidt's research with mediums (see above, p. 57).

[72] A fortress of the Hapsburgs during their repressive domination of Switzerland.

[73] As in the next dream.

[74] Meier, ed., *Atom and Archetype*, pp. 50f.

[75] In other words, behind the anima's perspective is the Blond (and the Persian, i.e., the Stranger) whose representative she is.

differently about the nature of nature, the makeup of matter and the state of science; and this pressure comes from the Blond. The Blond stands for a new "superior" understanding of life that will eventually coalesce into the Stranger in Pauli's dream landscape. This was what the flood has been about.

The eight keys at the end of the dream denote a hopeful aspect. Jung's extensive research has shown that the symbol of four and multiples of four represent completion; we can conclude from this, then, that there is a realistic possibility for Pauli to successfully conclude the challenge that the dream poses. With those keys, Pauli can open the door to a new understanding of the world. The fact that there are eight keys (two times four) stresses that Pauli is capable of completing the task that this and subsequent dreams announce.

## The Persian

The day prior to this dream of December 11, 1947 Pauli reports that he was feeling very depressed. Then came the dream:

> I arrive at my former house. I see how a dark-skinned young man in whom I recognize the Persian is putting objects into the house through the window. I make out a circular piece of wood and several letters. Then he approaches me in a friendly manner and I begin a conversation with him:
>
>     I: "You are not allowed to study?"
>
>     He: "No, therefore I study in secret."
>
>     I: "What subject are you studying?"
>
>     He: "Yourself!"
>
>     I: "You speak to me in a very sharp voice!"
>
>     He: "I speak as someone to whom everything else is forbidden."
>
>     I: "Are you my shadow?"
>
> He: "I am between you and the Light, so you are my shadow, not the reverse."

I: "Do you study physics?"

He: "There your language is too difficult for me, but in *my* language *you* do *not* understand physics!"[76]

I: "What are you doing here?"

He: "I am here to help you. You must give up a few illusions. For example, you believe that you have several women, but in reality you have only one. A moment ago I looked through the window and saw that you had no chair in your study. If you had said that to me, I could have smuggled a chair into your room today! But now I have to fetch one. I will hurry."[77]

The Persian is the other half of what will become the Stranger, the chthonic, natural aspect.[78] This means that where the blond man embodies the mental and intellectual understanding of the Stranger, the Persian portrays the instinctual and earthy experience of what the Stranger represents. Whereas the blond man refers to theoretical understanding, the Persian relates to practically living that point of view in daily life. The Blond represents a way of looking at things, the Persian a way of living that is consonant with the new standpoint. On a slightly more prosaic level the blond man represents how the mind grasps what the Stranger represents, the Persian how the body lives out that understanding. The Persian's aspect of things is more personal and more physical.

So the Persian, in a general sense and by comparison with the Blond, signifies the practical consequences for Pauli's lifestyle,[79] a

---

[76] Remember this voice is speaking to a Nobel laureate in physics!

[77] Van Erkelens, *Wolfgang Pauli*, p 52 (dream 9); van Erkelens, "The Spirit of Matter," *Psychological Perspectives*, vol. 24, pp. 36f.; van Erkelens, "Wolfgang Pauli and the Chinese *Anima* Figure," *Eranos Yearbook 1999*, pp. 24f.

[78] The term "chthonic" originally referred to those gods and goddesses in Greek mythology who lived beneath the surface of the earth, particularly Hades, Persephone, Poseidon, Hecate. In psychology it has come to mean "earthy," "instinctual," connected with our bodily desires and the power they can have over us.

[79] And of *our* lifestyle as well—to the extent that we, like Pauli, are still living within an old paradigm.

way of living, not just a way of hypothesizing. The Persian touches on Pauli's relation to instincts and erotic desire.

How important this is for Pauli is suggested by the Persian's saying that "I am between you and the Light." There is a source of new illumination within Pauli (the Light), and the Persian mediates that illumination to Pauli at a visceral level—in a way that goes to the very heart and bodily core of the man. Moreover, the Persian notices that there is no chair in Pauli's office. As we refer to a professor's position as a "chair" of a discipline at a university—Pauli had the chair of theoretical physics at the ETH—from the point of view of the Persian, Pauli does *not* have a "chair" of physics, and the Persian is willing to bring him one. This introduces the "new professorship" that will come up at the request of the Stranger. Another practical implication of the Persian is that he wants Pauli not just to understand a new point of view and live it practically and bodily; the Persian also wants Pauli to express it openly in his scientific work and in his role of professor. In the chair image the Persian is suggesting that Pauli begin to take up another perspective in his work as a scientist and to begin speaking openly about the new perspective that the blond man and the Persian—and soon the Stranger—are introducing him to.

The Persian is right to note the absence of the "chair" in Pauli's life. As far as the Persian is concerned, what Pauli was teaching— the fundamentals of quantum mechanics in a strictly academic sense—does not constitute Pauli's proper vocation. The Persian wants Pauli to widen the subject matter he articulates from his "chair" of physics, and hence the Persian offers to bring that new chair. Pauli was alluding to the same in his reference to the earlier dream of the Persian asking to be admitted to, "accepted into" the ETH. In this regard the Persian corresponds to the intent of a completely new point of view to be accepted into the world-view of science. The Persian's wish to be included in science is a representation of those kinds of forces that have moved science forward across the centuries. As far as the Persian is concerned, Pauli did not understand science, because the Persian is in touch with a knowledge of science far more extensive that that encompassed by the state of physics at that time. The Persian knows of future developments in science, so, by comparison, Pauli's grasp of scientific work is limited. The Persian is pointing with all his heart to the future; it is this world-view that the Blond and the Persian press Pauli to anticipate in his personal and professional life.

There is more to say about the Persian, but I believe these comments will make more sense after studying the Stranger's appearance in Pauli's inner world in the next dream. We will consider that dream and then continue elucidating the nature of this unconscious content that entered Pauli's life so insistently.

### The Stranger

Jung and Pauli talked on November 6, 1948, and their conversation involved a discussion about synchronicity, as is evident from Pauli's letter to Jung from November 7:

> Our talk yesterday on the "synchronicity" of dreams and external circumstances . . . was of great help to me, and I should like to thank you once again.[80]

On November 24, 1948, Pauli dreamed of the Stranger. This is the first appearance of the Stranger, and surely the figure's entry onto Pauli's dream stage can be seen as a response to the meeting with Jung two-and-a-half weeks earlier. From that time on Pauli no longer dreamed of the blond man or of the Persian, but rather of the Stranger who represents the synthesis of the two. Pauli stated that in this dream,

> a further transformation of the archetype, previously represented in the figures of the "Persian" and the "Blond," occurs through a reconciliation of the opposites light-dark. Since then the figure has appeared as one and the same man.[81]

---

[80] Meier, ed., *Atom and Archetype*, p. 34.

[81] Von Meyenn, ed., *Briefwechsel,* p. 257; van Erkelens, *Wolfgang Pauli,* p. 56.

The dream is as follows:

I see a river which flows from south to north, as does the Rhine. A dark man goes into the river and is swallowed up by it. In this moment "the mother" appears (only similar in features to my personal mother) and asks me what colors I have chosen. I respond by saying I have chosen "black-white." Immediately a hexagram appears with black and white stripes on a piece of paper (Figure 15), and the mother disappears.

Figure 15. Pauli's black and white stripes.

That is obviously a reference to the *I Ching's* hexagram one, Ch'ien, signifiying the creative power in the unconscious that begets in time.

Now a man with blond hair comes. A gush of air blows the piece of paper into his face, so that the stripe pattern remains marked on his nose. Next the man with the striped nose is startled as he observes three pieces of wood on the ground (Figure 16)

He reflects a moment, then appears to understand something and extends his hand out over the river. *Immediately a man comes out of the river*. He has black hair but a face bathed in light (with characteristics of the Persian, the Blond and the shadow).

Figure 16.
Three pieces of wood.

At that the man with the striped nose says to the other: "Do you know that you have lived before?" The one who came out of the river says, "No." The first says: "Everyone was shocked when you went into the river. But I noticed your postmortal effects, for example these three pieces of wood here. This gave me the certainty that you only appeared to be dead. The man answered, "Now I am beginning to remember something from before."

The man with the striped nose disappeared as well as the three pieces of wood. The man with the dark hair and illuminated face, who had come out of the river, alone remained. He seemed to be very happy to be back on land again.[82]

This is a very complicated dream and the focus here will be on examining its major features directly related to our theme.

The river in the dream flows from south to north, as the Rhine in fact does. Elsewhere in Pauli's writing and correspondence, he had described that for him the north means intuition. He had made up a sort of geographic schema as an association to some of the places in his dreams, with north being intuition and the south being sensation—this is easier to understand if we visualize him in Switzerland with sensuous Italy to his south and the far-sighted creativity of German culture to the north.[83] As intuition is the function of consciousness that has to do with sniffing things out and anticipating future possibilities, the flow of the river from south to

---

[82] Van Erkelens, *Wolfgang Pauli*, p. 56 (dream 10).

[83] Meier, ed., *Atom and Archetype*, p. 123; Enz, *Pauli hat gesagt*, p. 113.

which are moving from the present into the future—just as I have proposed that the Persian's being illuminated indicated a far-reaching knowledge. The dream is looking to the future.

The dream's broadest lines involve the transformation of the dark man who appears at the beginning: he opens the dream, then goes into the river and, at the end, emerges as a mixture of the Persian and the Blond. Thus the dream concerns his evolution.

The evolution of the dark man corresponds to the evolution of Pauli's own understanding of synchronicity, as well as of the relationship between spirit and matter, inner and outer. The two poles, the Peersian and Blond, are represented in the dream: the dark man at the beginning and the blond man who comes along. The end of the dream, then, synthesizes the two into a unified figure. This means that the discussion of synchronicity with Jung had the effect of clarifying Pauli's perception of the spirit-matter issue into a cohesive one. That there were previously two figures in Pauli's dream life circumscribing the unity of spirit and matter shows that Pauli was split in his understanding. He had been willing to grant the theoretical existence of this unity but in fact did not really accept the practical consequences of what that unity means for the Occidental value system and certainly did not grant what that unity meant in his personal life. He was fascinated with the idea of the unity of matter and spirit but was not willing to live it. Certainly the former is documented throughout his correspondence with Jung, and the latter is something we will shortly see manifesting in his life.

Thus the dream shows us a synthesis in Pauli's understanding of matter and spirit. That the Blond, the Persian and the Stranger are pointing toward the spirit-matter problem is confirmed by the appearance of just those images in Pauli's dream a fortnight after his discussion with Jung. The images' connection to Pauli and Jung's conversation at the beginning of November, as well as Pauli's own comments on the images, demonstrates their meaning.

The descent into the river takes place in the presence of "the mother." Jung has referred to the "maternal intellect" as being the hallmark of a creative personality. In his memorial tribute to Richard Wilhelm, the man who sent him *The Secret of the Golden Flower*, Jung said:

> As a rule the specialist's is a purely masculine mind, an intellect to which fecundity is an alien and unnatural process; it is therefore an especially ill-adapted tool for giving rebirth to a foreign spirit. But a larger mind bears the stamp of the feminine; it is endowed with a receptive and fruitful womb which can reshape what is strange and give it a familiar form. Wilhelm possessed the rare gift of a maternal intellect.[84]

The presence of the mother, therefore, indicates that Pauli should develop a maternal intellect in order to synthesize his understanding of the unity of matter and spirit, both as regards his mental understanding of it and as regards his ability to live in his own life what his destiny was asking of him. Naturally, as a physicist, Pauli's mind was that of a specialist, but the dream emphasizes the maternal intellect's fecundity in receiving and reshaping, in giving rebirth to, a new way of seeing and living, a reshaping which takes what is strange and makes it familiar so that it can live on into the future.

Pauli's choice of black and white and the appearance of the *I Ching's* hexagram number one affects the blond man, as can be seen when the stripes stick to his nose. The *I Ching* is a book of Chinese oracles whereby, through a procedure of throwing coins or picking up sticks, six different "lines" are created, either broken or solid. The coins or sticks register the quality of the moment and provide the questioner an answer to some problem that is weighing on his or her soul. In creating a pattern of six different lines, either broken or solid, the questioner generates a response which then can be compared with commentary from the text of the *I Ching* concerning the meaning of the pattern or hexagram. The commentary in the *I Ching* is then taken as the oracular response to

---

[84] "Richard Wilhelm: In Memoriam," *The Spirit in Man, Art, and Literature,* CW 15, par.76.

the question posed.

The hexagram made up of six solid lines is called the "Creative." It refers to the creative powers of the universe coming to the aid of the questioner. Hexagram number one advises the questioner that the issue brought to the oracle for advice will be addressed (often from the outside world) by creative powers.[85] Therefore the hexagram flying onto the nose (sniffing out!) of the blond man, the figure that represents the intellectual understanding of the spirit-matter issue, suggests that this understanding is being impressed with the reality of creative powers of a larger magnitude. When the hexagram sticks to the nose of the blond man, Pauli's intellectual understanding is being shaken up as it confronts a principle in life that is bigger, more pervasive and more profound than anything the mind can grasp. This is just another way of saying that the dream is about the transformation of Pauli's understanding of the connection between spirit and matter.

The three pieces of wood enter the dream at the disappearance of the dark man into the river. They are the "postmortal effects" of the man who goes into the river; that is, they are a manifestation of the man who is being reborn into the image of the Stranger. In other words, the dream indicates that the three pieces of wood are another form of the Stranger. This has to do with the lower trinity.

Jung's study of images of God in pre-Christian belief systems shows that most early religions symbolize God with images that are made up of four parts or multiples of four parts. Jung considered such images to be a full representation of divinity, whereas the great limitation of Christianity was that it was able to symbolize God only in terms of three, cutting off one-fourth of what God had previously been considered to be. In a way this made sense for the times in which Christianity was born, because life had become so wild and desperate—the despair, hedonism and brutality of late antiquity—that the prevailing view of life had to be shrunk down in order to stabilize civilization. This is Jung's view put very simply,

---

[85] Richard Wilhelm, trans., *The I Ching or Book of Changes*, pp. 3ff.

but adequate for our purposes here. Suffice it to say that partly for understandable reasons but also for ones that have now become problematic,[86] the Christian representation of God has cut out a quarter of what earlier religions considered to be divine. So the Christian God is a Trinity where previously God had been a quaternity. The tripartite quality of the Christian God has left out an important part of life, and what has been left out often appears in myths, fairy tales and dreams not as a missing "one," as we might think, but as another type of triple image containing all that the Christian image lacks. Whereas the three of the Christian God is spirit—Father, Son and Holy Spirit as ethereal beings who live in heaven—the other three image is material—we could say Mother, Daughter and Earthly spirit. And just as the upper Trinity—Father, Son and Holy Spirit—is thought to represent the guiding function of divinity, so in myth, fairy tales and dreams the lower trinity is also often depicted as a guide capable of leading a person. And just as the upper Trinity is thought to manifest in spiritual experience, so the lower trinity is depicted as manifesting in earthly or material (chthonic) experience. Accordingly, the lower trinity encompasses the same guiding power as the upper Trinity, but since it is "lower" it signifies that there are also guiding experiences to be had in relation to the material aspects of life, not just in relation to the ones nominally considered spiritual.

Pauli linked the three pieces of wood in the dream to the lower trinity.[87] This certainly makes sense because the lower trinity, the potential guiding function of certain physical experiences, concerns the nature of synchronicity. In synchronicity we reevaluate our understanding of spirit and matter and see the guiding or symbolic capacity of matter, that is of events in the physical world. The allusion to the lower trinity in the dream, and the way the lower trinity has appeared in myth, fairy tales and dreams throughout the ages, is further evidence that we are on the right track in following

---

[86] This will be discussed in greater detail in the last chapter.

[87] Meier, ed., *Atom and Archetype*, pp. 49f.

Pauli's understanding of the Stranger. Through his association to the lower trinity, the Stranger clearly embodies the link between spirit and matter and the creative power of images manifesting in matter, such as they do in a synchronicity.

Pauli referred to the Stranger as a dream form of Mercury and Mercurius. Who were they?

Mercurius is a figure that played a large role in alchemy. The alchemists imagined the transformation of their base material in mythological terms, and one of the key images they used to personify the substance on which they worked was Mercurius. He was thought to represent all phases of the alchemical process: he was the beginning phase of the material and he was also the end point, and he was the means whereby the material went from the beginning to the end state.[88] Mercurius was clearly related to the God Hermes in ancient Greece and to Hermes' Roman counterpart, Mercury. Hermes/Mercury lent himself perfectly to representing the alchemical substance and its transformation because Mercury was a messenger who traveled from place to place carrying the missives of the gods. He could thus aptly be modified slightly in the mind of the alchemists to symbolize the "soul" of the material they were measuring, chopping and cooking. They imagined there was something in matter itself which, from a beginning state, traveled through different forms until finally it reached the end state. At that point Mercurius became a representation of the goal of the alchemical opus.

Particularly important for our discussion is that Mercurius was considered to be both material and spiritual. Jung writes:

> The oldest reference to the mercurial *pneuma*[89] occurs in a . . . quotation of considerable antiquity (possibly pre-Christian), which says: "Go to the streamings of the Nile, and there you will find a stone that has a spirit." [90]

---

[88] "The Spirit Mercurius," *Alchemical Studies*, CW 13, par. 283.

[89] *Pneuma* is the Greek word for spirit.

[90] "The Spirit Mercurius," *Alchemical Studies*, CW 13, par. 265.

Mercurius circumscribes the transformative principle within the human psyche that becomes active when we reflect on ourselves. Jung, of course, studied the work of the alchemists as a metaphor for inner processes which occur during healing and growth. The process of transformation that the alchemists thought they were accomplishing literally, Jung saw as symbolic of the process of psychological transformation in personal healing. Mercurius, who is the beginning, middle and end of a physical evolution in matter, as the alchemists saw it, became for Jung a depiction of the beginning, middle and end of a process of psychological development.

As a metaphor, Mercurius represents the knowledge and forward movement toward consciousness that seeks—though we may not be aware of it—to unfold in all our emotional suffering. Mercurius personifies the healing activity of our psyche, a goal-seeking drive to health that resides in all of us and silently directs us toward greater consciousness. Mercurius is a personification of the inborn capacity of this meaningful unfolding that, when we understand it and cooperate with it, forms the backdrop of our growth. And do not forget that for the alchemist Mercurius is both physical and spiritual; he is a mixture of opposites that disregards concepts of "inner" and "outer," "material" and "spiritual." He is simply inside and outside, according to the alchemist. Jung understood this metaphorically: the dynamics of growth are likewise not limited to either inner or outer, subject or object, psychological space or material world. That is the essence of the psychoid archetype

Jung felt that the figure of Mercurius, like the lower trinity, also aptly symbolized the part of the psyche that had happily escaped the influence of Christian civilization:

> In comparison with the purity and unity of the Christ symbol, Mercurius-lapis is ambiguous, dark, paradoxical, and thoroughly pagan. It therefore represents a part of the psyche which was certainly not moulded by Christianity and can on no account be expressed by the symbol "Christ." . . . The paradoxical nature of Mercurius reflects an important aspect of the self—the fact, namely,

that he is essentially a *complexio oppositorum*, and indeed can be nothing else if it is to represent any kind of totality.[91]

That passage conveys the ambiguity of the Mercurial process. Whereas the Christian idea of redemption is purely light, the ambiguous nature of Mercurius indicates that all sorts of emotional complications and dubious moral tones will accompany the process of transformation that he signifies. When the spirit of growth manifests in the physical world, when synchronistic experiences embroil us in the affairs of matter, there are bound to be moral complications and waves of heartache. Insofar as the Stranger becomes active in Pauli's life, it will be no surprise to find this as a characteristic of what draws Pauli in. This is the spirit's dark aspect that Pauli wished to avoid. No wonder he was so ready to take the matter-spirit issue as a theoretical fancy. Howver, it seems that, out of Pauli's conversation with Jung in November, he was beginning to realize the complicated nature of the spirit-matter unity. The Persian as the earthy side of the guiding spirit, symbolizing the fact that the material world becomes our directive, was thus being united with a theoretical understanding of the possibility of the unity of matter and spirit at this point in Pauli's life, through the discussion with Jung. The Stranger, like Mercurius, embodies challenges both to our way of understanding and to our way of living. Pauli would soon be meeting this ambiguity of the lower trinity and Mercurius in his personal life.

Let us return for a moment to the Persian. Earlier I suggested it would be helpful to examine the Stranger before trying to grasp some of the characteristics of what the Persian signified. In a way, we have been talking about the Persian all along in our discussion of the Stranger, since the Persian is simply the aspect of the Stranger that is tied to the material world, while the Blond represents the mental or theoretical understanding of these matters.

---

[91] Ibid., par. 289. Mercurius-lapis stresses that he is also the goal; *lapis*, or stone, was a word the alchemists used for the final product of their work. *Complexio oppositorum* means a mixture of opposites.

But unlike the detached Blond who can understand without the heat of strong emotions, the Persian brings with him all kinds of passions since his is the recognition of the unity of matter and spirit in daily life. Now, hopefully, it is clear what was meant by some of the earlier inferences of the Persian: that he was forbidden in Pauli's life—in so far as Pauli would have preferred to understand these questions mentally only; that he was between Pauli and the light—he was meant to convey a new understanding to Pauli of the nature of reality at the visceral level; that he tells Pauli that Pauli does not understand physics—again a reference to Pauli wanting to keep the spirit-matter problem theoretical; that he made a comment to Pauli concerning his relation to women—this will of course be the place where Pauli meets the complications of Mercurius.

There is still a lingering question concerning the Persian. Why did Pauli's dreams choose the image of the Persian to convey these points? Why a Persian, exactly? Pauli did not offer associations or comment on this question, but it warrants consideration.

The Persian that played such a role in Jung's psychological work was Zarathustra—as he appears in Nietzsche's *Thus Spake Zarathustra*, written over several years beginning in 1883.[92] Jung devoted some years to an interpretation of this work in an English seminar and discussed just a little over half of the book before World War Two intervened and the seminar had to be cancelled.

Jung repeatedly expressed his opinion on the importance of Nietzsche's work, saying in a letter that he felt Nietzsche was crucial to an understanding of modern life since he tackled issues that no one else had.[93] Nietzsche had taught Classics at the university in Basel where Jung was raised and while Jung was very young; Nietzsche then took up an itinerant lifestyle traveling between the Swiss alps, the French Riviera and northern Italy

---

[92] *Nietzsche's* Zarathustra: *Notes of the Seminar Given in 1934 – 1939*, vol. 1, p. 10.

[93] "Nietzsche was to me the only man of that time who gave some adequate answers to certain urgent questions which then were more felt than thought." *Letters*, vol. 2, p. 622.

where he eked out a miserably poor life devoted to his writing. His work was viciously ignored in his own time. Yet, one of the great classicists of the early twentieth century, F.M. Cornford, wrote of Nietzsche in 1912 that he "left the scholarship of a generation toiling in the rear."[94]

Zarathustra (ca. 600 BCE) was the prophet of ancient Persian Zoroastrianism.[95] He introduced the idea of the cosmic struggle of good and evil into the arena of world religion. In Zoroastrianism the universe consists of an ongoing battle between a good God (Ahura Mazda or Ormazd) and an evil one (Angro Mainyush or Ahriman).[96] As Jung spoke of Zarathustra in the seminar:

> His teaching was the cosmic struggle between the powers of light and darkness, and he it was who perpetuated this eternal conflict.[97]

The influence of this on Christianity is obvious. Jung said Zarathustra was "really the real founder of the Christian dogma."[98] Influenced by the metaphysics of Zoroastrianism, Christianity was likewise a religion emphasizing the struggle between the powers of good and evil; and Christian morality, like Zoroastrian morality, involved behaving well for the rewards of the good God. Both are "religions of rewards" where people "are good only in order to be rewarded in heaven."[99]

Zarathustra, then, ushered in some of the essential vision of Christianity which has also become central to the Western world-view. In Zoroastrianism there is a clear distinction between good and evil, with good connected with the heavenly spiritual powers constantly threatened by evil. In terms of our discussion, Zarathustra was the originator of the split between spirit and matter,

---

[94] Bernd Magnus, "Friedrich Nietzsche," in *Encyclopædia Britannica 2003 Deluxe Edition.*

[95] Zarathustra is the Persian name; Zoroaster is the Greek version.

[96] *Nietzsche's* Zarathustra, vol. 1, pp. 5ff.

[97] Ibid., p. 5.

[98] Ibid., p. 8.

[99] Ibid.

gladly adopted and espoused by Christendom in particular, and then later by the West in general, since the good and evil of Zoroastrianism easily became the spirit and matter of our own civilization. In Nietzsche's work, itself prompted by dreams of Zarathustra,[100] Zarathustra returns to set right the error he had introduced into civilization two-and-a-half millennia ago. Nietzsche wrote:

> Zarathustra was the first to see in the struggle between good and evil the essential wheel in the working of things. . . . Zarathustra created the most portentous error, morality. Consequently he should also be the first to perceive that error.[101]

In *Thus Spake Zarathustra*, then, the Persian returns. He begins to descend from his forest retreat, and the first thing he sees on his way out of is an old saint who had also retired there. Jung interprets the descent of Zarathustra in a vein similar to what Nietzsche just mentioned: Zarathustra, representing the impulse which created Christian consciousness, fell from view after the birth of our civilization and is now returning to correct the errors he introduced. He sees the old saint who signifies the moribund and overly spiritual nature of Christianity which, in its present form, has long outlasted its usefulness but endures as a sort of ostrich, apart from the real needs of the world and oblivious to its circumstances. It is at this point in the narrative that Nietzsche issues his famous statement through the voice of Zarathustra:

> When Zarathustra was alone, however, he said to his heart: "Could it be possible! This old saint in the forest hath not yet heard of it, that *God is dead!*"[102]

Throughout the book Zarathustra proclaims and describes the new world which he has come to announce and which will replace the one reigned over by the Christian God. As Zarathustra first

---

[100] Ibid., pp. 3f. and n. 2.

[101] Ibid., p. 5.

[102] Nietzsche, *Thus Spake Zarathustra*, p. 6.

represented an impetus to the values on which the last two thousand years of Western Christian civilization are based, in his return he symbolizes the impetus to the values which will be the foundation of the next epoch.

To Jung's mind, Nietzsche's work articulates the forces shaping our world. That is to say his work is truly prophetic. Jung felt that Nietzsche's description of Zarathustra represented the dynamism deep within the human species that is giving rise to our historical change. The Christian epoch is dying, and a new one, personified by Zarathustra, is coming into existence. In Nietzsche's work, Zarathustra's utterances are descriptions of the psychology of the times as the world leaves the protective shelter of the Christian world-view.

Those features of Zarathustra's world to come bring us right back to the theme of spirit and matter which has been our focus. Zarathustra emphasizes the death of a spirituality which lives apart from the world, and he stresses a new set of values concerning the sacredness of the earth and the earthy:

> Once blasphemy against God was the greatest blasphemy; but God died, and therewith also those blasphemers. To blaspheme the earth is now the dreadfulest sin, and to rate the heart of the unknowable higher than the meaning of the earth![103]

So Zarathustra, the Persian, is a portrait of a new orientation of humanity, a new ethic as well, which is based on the development of human passion, understanding and integrity.

"The meaning of the earth!" Could there be a clearer expression of why the dark figure in Pauli's dream is a Persian!? The Persian, when seen against the backdrop of Nietzsche's work, carries a far greater significance than anything Pauli's own personal psychology could conjure up. The task of the Persian—and his later form the Stranger—stands for Pauli's fear of the demands of flesh and matter, it is true; but these inner figures also point to the surfacing of a historical development in Pauli's personal dream life, an

---

[103] Ibid., p. 7.

example of what Jung means by the collective unconscious. Our personal problems are often not only our own; they may also signal developments in culture and history such that our individual struggle is a manifestation of a larger process in a wider context. In this sense the Persian, and the Stranger, are an example of Pauli's being tapped to participate in new psychological developments as much as they are also indicative of his personal dilemmas.

The spirit and matter issue is something we are all being called to face. The task of our time is to make life in time and space, the relationship to the physical events in life, the sacred altar of being.[104] Zarathustra is a personification of what moves us as lust for the world eclipses the self-righteous and sky-oriented excesses of Christianity. In the modern era, for more and more people, engagement with the world has replaced spirituality. This is both a danger and an opportunity. It is a danger because humanity could fall back into a decadence as destructive as the Roman one. It is an opportunity because there is a spirit within that lust which, if found, can lead the way toward transformation. Thus the Persian and the Stranger—and also Zarathustra's return—suggest that the material world and physical events can be understood in a wider significance. The death of the old spirituality and the birth of a new materiality summon us to find guidance in a new place; the death of the old God must be made creative. This is the responsibility history has placed on our shoulders. We are being called to move forward through chaos.

Persia was renamed Iran in 1935; now the name of the Persian reminds us that we have landed right in the chaos of contemporary history. Of course Zoroastrianism is not Islam, yet they both grew on the same soil, Islam eventually taking the place of its more ancient predecessor. Is it mere coincidence that the Persian is trying

---

[104] Another visionary of our era, Teilhard de Chardin, saw Christ descend and become the world. This occurred during the hell of the Battle of Verdun while Teilhard, a Jesuit priest, was serving in the French trenches as a medic. (Ursula King, *Spirit of Fire: The Life and Vision of Teilhard de Chardin*, p. 60) The Church silenced Teilhard's theological writings.

to reach Pauli and, in the next dream, is setting fires while today a fiery conflict that threatens the stability of the world is raging in the Middle East as finally the United States has met its formidable foe? Or is it a fateful instance of synchronicity?

The now-deceased Egyptian, Arabic philosopher Sayyid Qutb, has been called "the brains behind bin Laden."[105] He is the philosopher on whose work bin Laden bases his vendetta against the West. Qutb's complaint about the West is that it separates the religious and the secular, or we might say spirit and matter. In this he is voicing typical Islamic theology:

> The spiritual realization of the right relationship between God and the individual sanctifies all of life. . . . The whole world, material and spiritual, body and soul, is created by God, and every sphere of human action has a moral and spiritual dimension. The secular cannot be separated from the religious within Islam; everything is ultimately religious, because everything proceeds from God and belongs to Him. . . . The modern inclination to separate state and religion is entirely foreign to Islamic tradition. A Muslim cannot say, "Give to Caesar what is Caesar's and to God what is God's," because everything is God's. Life is an integrated whole and all of it must be lived as an act of service to God."[106]

This is not the place to debate the fine points of the Islamic viewpoint versus Western-style capitalistic democracy. I do not wish to condone the violence of Islamic fundamentalism, as I also do not wish to condone the shortsightedness of American foreign policy with its self-righteous and imperialistic flavor. But if we can look beyond the particulars of the argument to see that the message of Islam—whatever criticisms we may have of its fundamentalist interpretations, excesses and limitations—with a slight shift in perspective can be understood in a way not unlike the message of Nietzsche's Zarathustra. The thrust of both of them, and a point of

---

[105] *The Diane Rehm Show*, NPR, March 26, 2003; *All Things Considered*, NPR, May 6, 2003.

[106] John M. Koller and Patricia Joyce Koller, *Asian Philosophies*, pp. 94ff.

view certainly contrary to the prevailing world-view of both Western science and religion, is that there needs to be a reevaluation of the split between spirit and matter. Seen in this light it is no surprise that the Persian is knocking on our door, from the incredibly far-seeing insights of Friedrich Nietzsche to the dreams of a physicist disillusioned with the science he had made his first love, to a factor now returning to us through the grief and disorientation of a war with fundamentalist Islam.

## The assignment

Two more of Pauli's dreams will conclude this chapter. The Stranger is a true symbol;[107] he personifies a knowledge that we are just beginning to fathom. We will have to live with him so that he can slowly communicate his point of view. He was present in Pauli's dreams with a meaning for Pauli, of course, but beyond that his existence goes beyond Pauli's personal life and reaches out for understanding from all of us.

The Stranger was asking Pauli for a personal response to his issue and its relation to our time, as the following dreams will indicate. As before, the dreams are filled with detail that would yield a rich psychological harvest, but here only their broadest meaning as it relates to our theme will be explored.

The first dream is from October 6, 1949:

> I am with colleagues on one of the upper floors of a house where a local conference on mathematics and physics is being held. I see that under my name a course of *cookery* is announced: "Start: December 15." Surprised, I ask a young man near me why the course begins so late in the year. He answers: "Because then the Nobel prize will be granted."[108]

---

[107] A symbol is a picture of something as of yet not completely knowable. A sign is a veiled expression of something knowable or already known. For instance, Jung thought Freud's use of the term "phallic symbol" would better be called a "phallic sign," since it expresses something knowable, just usually hidden from view.

[108] The Swiss academic year starts in October. Pauli had received the Nobel Prize four years earlier.

Now I notice that a *fire* has started in the adjacent room. I take fright (*affect*), run down a staircase among many floors (*panic*). Finally I succeed in getting outside. Looking back, I see that two floors of the house, where the colleagues were gathered, are burnt down. I walk across the level ground and enter a *garage*. I see that a taxi is waiting for me and that the taxi driver fills the tank with petrol. I look more closely: I recognize "him," the light-dark "stranger." Immediately I feel secure. "Probably *he* has lighted the fire," I think, without saying it aloud.

He says to me quietly: "Now we can refuel, because upstairs there has been a fire. I will take you where you belong!" Then he drives me off.[109]

The image of the fire is central; a few comments on the outline of the dream will place the fire in context.

The dream starts on the upper floor of a conference on mathematics and physics. The upper floor would suggest being above reality, above the emotional demands of life. Jung, interpreting a dream of Pauli's from the time of his personal crisis in 1932, comments that Pauli was a man who "always tried to evade his emotional needs. . . . All this had nothing to do with science or an academic career."[110]

Most likely the locale of the dream, the upper floor of a mathematics and physics atmosphere, refers to Pauli's tendency to flee emotional chaos by taking refuge in the impersonal objectivity of academic science. The reference to cooking would exemplify transformation, changing substances from one state to another, while cooking in the emotional juices that usually belong to such undertakings. The substance to be cooked was Pauli himself, away from his aloof rationality and toward a more down-to-earth emotionality. His cooking was to take him away from the standard

---

[109] van Erkelens, *Wolfgang Pauli*, p. 64 (dream 13); van Erkelens, "The Spirit of Matter," *Psychological Perspectives*, 24, p. 39.

[110] "Psychology and Religion," *Psychology and Religion*, CW 11, par. 72. That the published dreams in this long essay belong to Pauli is confirmed in Meier, ed., *Atom and Archetype*, p. 10.

model of academic science which still splits spirit and matter and which still has no means for conceptualizing, much less acknowledging, the emotional significance of those moments when matter does act in a symbolic fashion. The Stranger, at the back of all this, has started the fire. At the end of the dream the Stranger will take Pauli to where Pauli belongs, that is, to his real self and the real work he is to accomplish at the Stranger's bidding— articulating a new point of view.

The Stranger has lighted the fire to bring Pauli down to emotional earth in order to lead him to a recognition and completion of his real task in becoming a spokesperson for the Stranger. The Stranger's reality as envoy of the unity of spirit and matter wants to be expressed to others, and Pauli is to attend to the Stranger's reality, intent and knowledge.

Pauli was soon to experience this fire in a human relationship. His contact with Marie-Louise von Franz began in the early 1940s when Pauli was working on his Kepler article.[111] At the end of 1950 von Franz sent Pauli a copy of a manuscript in which she had interpreted an alchemical text, and shortly thereafter the two of them began a personal relationship characterized by a considerable intensity.[112] It is difficult to know just exactly what the emotional nature of the relationship was. One author has called it an "intellectual love affair" while another has referred to Pauli's attraction to von Franz as a "transference."[113] Pauli's last assistant and biographer, Charles Enz, said of an important communiqué sent to von Franz by Pauli, "Certainly love was involved in that.[114] But however we wish to label their rapport, it is clear that there was a burning fire between them. They spent time together discussing personal matters, their dreams, Jungian psychology, this issue of

---

[111] Enz, *Pauli hat gesagt*, p. 114.

[112] van Erkelens, *Wolfgang Pauli*, p. 75.

[113] David Lindorff, *Pauli and Jung*, p. 152; van Erkelens, *Wolfgang Pauli*, pp. 77ff.

[114] Ikon Television, *The Psychology of Jung: Passions of the Soul, Mind and Matter*.

spirit and matter, science and religion, and so on. In addition, a lively correspondence flourished at points in their fascination with each other. The relation developed more fully in 1951, but then it eventually dwindled until Pauli's death in 1958, with von Franz becoming more and more frustrated by Pauli's progressive emotional aloofness.

Most of von Franz's letters to Pauli apparently have not survived, though his to her have. In copies of his letters to von Franz which are in my possession, he ends with *"Alles Liebe und Gute"*— ("All love and all the best.").[115] In another letter he writes that they should have a spiritual love and not a physical love together.[116] Surely, if there had been no fire between them, Pauli would not have felt it necessary to say what should not be. Other indications of their emotional closeness can be found in the correspondence. Pauli wrote: "Monday was wonderful,"[117] "I am beginning to suffer because of the long separation from you,"[118] "With sincere thanks for much soul help."[119] In a correspondence that did survive from von Franz, she wrote: "Your letter made me very happy, I again have the feeling of a strong connection with you."[120]

It is neither my purpose here nor my interest to dissect their emotional relationship. Suffice it to say there were strong feelings between them and certainly their statements to each other attest to an erotic component to the friendship. Each must have touched the mind and soul of the other. This eros is the fire in the dream that was to bring Pauli down to his emotions and to the task that the Stranger was, in effect, taking him to at the end of the dream. The

---

[115] For example, dated June 20, 1951; I thank David Lindorff for graciously sharing this information.

[116] van Erkelens, *Wolfgang Pauli*, p. 81.

[117] Ibid., p. 91.

[118] Ibid., p. 93.

[119] Ibid., p. 122.

[120] Ibid., p. 134.

Stranger started the fire, which means that this aspect of Pauli's personality was arranging an erotic presence in his life for the purpose of propelling Pauli into his true work. He was not only to grapple with the reality of the unity of matter and spirit in science, or in Western understanding in general, but also in the demands his own life placed on him as he sought to be true to what his heart and body wanted. As the relation to von Franz was most likely the place where Pauli experienced the fire that the Stranger set, her presence in his life was thus to aid him in completing his work with and for the Stranger.

What a perfect partner fate placed before him! Grounded in Jungian psychology's theory and practice like few others, interested in and familiar with the issues around quantum physics' challenge to the Western definition of reality, with a brilliant intellect matched by an emotional availability and depth, von Franz was perhaps one of the few, or maybe the only one, who could have worked with Pauli in depth and supported his creativity along the lines of the Stranger. Conversely, Pauli was in a position to be of tremendous help to her as they could collaborate on these problems of spirit and matter, psychology and science, perhaps publishing— with him contributing his knowledge of science and interest in Jungian psychology to her knowledge of Jungian psychology and interest in science. His prestige in the field of science would have opened the door for their work to the world at large

The Stranger provided Pauli with the love capable of supporting and sustaining his new assignment, and then the Stranger began to announce that very challenge in dreams. The next dream, from December 9, 1951, is an example of the Stranger's offerings for the deeper course of Pauli's creative life:

> I am on a ship and a very strong storm is raging. On the outboard of the ship stands the Stranger as a large, dark man. He is roping up and making arrangements to jump in the stormy sea. I at first think this is just sport, but he calls to me that he wants to retrieve a person out of the sea (NB, he does not say whether man or woman). Then completing his preparation he jumps into the ocean and I don't see

him any longer.

I then go into a large room in the ship, a kind of salon or sitting room. I see that a sort of official meeting is taking place there in order to choose a new professor. The result of the vote, which I am able to hear through the tumult of voices, is a man named "*Peter Strom.*"

He enters and has a completely misshapen figure, in particular an oddly flattened head, like this (Figure 17)—and all horizontal dimensions are strongly elongated. He has certain features of the dark man who jumped into the water. ...

I see that he has cleaved in two, though not completely. In the front he is a dark man, but in the back a very beautifully bright woman shines through quite distinctly. The two are very similar, like siblings—connected together in the middle of their bodies.[121]

Figure 17. Peter Strom.

Restricting ourselves to the main point of the dream as it applies to our theme, observe that it shows another transformation in which the Stranger is involved. Although the dream does not say so exactly, it is a fair assumption that the Stranger is going into the stormy sea—the storm of emotions that buffeted Pauli in his

---

[121] Van Erkelens, *Wolfgang Pauili*, pp. 100f. (dream 27). The remainder of the dream concerns separating the two bodies.

personal crisis with science and the feelings he had for Marie-Louise von Franz—to fetch "Peter Strom" out of the water.

Peter Strom is to be chosen the new professor. The new professor is another image of the new professorship, the new "chair" that Pauli was to initiate, literally incorporating the point of view of the Stranger in his courses at the ETH. The new professor—a theme that appears repeatedly in Pauli's dreams—represents a practical request. Pauli was to offer courses at the ETH on the limitations of the scientific model, for example on the challenge of synchronicity to the scientific paradigm, and so on. Peter Strom represents the rock solid personal commitment, as well as the flow and flexibility, required for the fulfillment of the new professorship (Peter is the "rock," and *Strom* means "stream" in German.)[122] Obviously those traits in Pauli are still in need of significant psychological work, as can be observed from the bizarre form of Peter Strom at the end of the dream.

The chair of physics, missing in the dream of the Persian, has returned. Pauli's task is clearly announced to him, and the Stranger seems so invested in its completion that he even provided Pauli with just the right partner to support the work as well as the fire to rivet Pauli to her.

**"It makes me sad"**

The sad part of my narrative is that Pauli never fulfilled his promise, his destiny. As early as 1932, Pauli had dreamed of his tendency to avoid the complications of his strong emotions and heard a voice say at the end of a dream: "The fire that is not put out is a holy fire."[123] Jung's commentary to the dream stated that Pauli was afraid his emotional needs "might get him into trouble" and that Pauli had a tendency "to run away from his adventure."[124] And run away he did, this time from his adventure with Marie-Louise

---

[122] Ibid., p. 101 and n. 15; van Erkelens credits Marie-Louise von Franz for this interpretation.

[123] "Psychology and Religion," *Psychology and Religion*, CW 11, par. 58.

[124] Ibid., pars. 72, 74.

von Franz. Although the relationship started with fire, Pauli eventually distanced himself from it and from her over time until mere pleasantries existed between them. Von Franz spoke of their relationship in a 1990 interview:

> I saw that he had lost the inner way. You don't know what is going to happen, but something horrible is going to happen. Later it turned out to be cancer. . . .
>
> The whole thing makes me sad. If you want me to sum up the relationship: I tried to pull him out and didn't succeed. ...
>
> He always scoffed at the feminine in his personal relationships, in his feeling. Like many intellectuals. . . .
>
> At that time I took a lot of trouble. He was a very tiring discussion partner, because he was quick and profound and intense. We generally walked about two or three hours in the woods. And then I was exhausted. . . .
>
> I sometimes made scenes, when I thought he was really on the wrong track. Then he just made joking remarks that I looked prettier the more I was angry. He didn't take it seriously. I banged on the table and said: I mean it seriously. It is a dangerous point. But he just scoffed at it. . . .
>
> He moved in the higher circles in physics. They were very mocking and cynical and jealous . . . . (of his Nobel prize). If he had stood up for dreams and irrational things, there would have been hellish laughter. And he hadn't the guts to face it. So that was really tragic.[125]

It is indeed sad that Pauli avoided his "assignment"; that is, he did not seriously take up the challenge of the new professorship. He failed in his relationship with von Franz, the one person who could most have helped him. Pauli was to represent the Stranger's point of view and convey it to public consciousness. At the Stranger's prompting, Pauli was to have placed the dialogue between the contemporary scientific world-view and the Stranger's point of view into a public forum. He was to have investigated all of the

---

[125] Van Erkelens, "Wolfgang Pauli, the Feminine and the Perils of the Modern Soul," *Harvest: Journal for Jungian Studies*, vol. 48, no.2, pp. 143ff.

implications of that dialogue for the way we, the West, view life. He was to have discussed repercussions of the Stranger's point of view that affect our lifestyle. He was, above all, to have experienced the unity of spirit and matter when the longing of his heart and body meaningfully placed him next to just the one woman who could understand and respond to his new professorship.[126] The hope expressed in Pauli's first dream that we discussed (portrayed in the image of the eight keys; above, page 83), was never brought to fruition in the man's life.

Though Pauli himself was not able fully to respond to the promptings of the Stranger, still his dreams give us, from another and important perspective, an additional view of the Stranger and his similarities to Mercurius: his duality on many fronts, his chthonic character, the superiority of his hidden knowledge and his utterly nonrational nature.

Remember what it was that motivated Pauli to turn back to his unconscious this second time around. He asked his unconscious what had gone wrong. How had science gotten off track? The answer from the unconscious was that science, indeed Western understanding, had gotten off track because it failed to investigate the unity of matter and spirit and to concede the point of view of the Stranger. Apparently the solution to the destructive power drive of science, at least in part, is that science begin to develop a paradigm that admits and takes seriously that there is such a thing as meaning in matter, that there is such a thing as archetypes in matter, that there is an intelligent relationship between the two parts of life that we have artificially separated, that determinative causality is of no value in discerning those moments when matter acts meaningfully.

Why this is so is certainly not immediately obvious. Why would

---

[126] In 1954 Pauli dreamed he was presented with a bill to pay, and then in the dream he ate beautiful red cherries from an envelope marked "philosophical choral society." Jung's comment is instructive: "It is typical of you to choose to convert the envelope with the red cherries into music, whereas I am afraid that is meant in very specific terms." (Meier, ed., *Atom and Archetype*, pp. 138, 155) Other dreams from this period confirm the same. See van Erkelens, *Wolfgang Pauli*, ch. 6.

the recognition of meaning in matter tame the destructiveness of science? A full answer to this question may lie in the future, as continued dialogue with the Stranger manifests more of his point of view and uncovers deeper inroads into his way of seeing. But surely it is important to address the question, even though our knowledge of the Stranger is still quite new.

The experience of synchronicity dethrones the arrogant subjectivity so typical of Western consciousness. When we realize that the outer world is also a subject and when we experience our own personality being reoriented through the meaningful activity of material events in the outer world, we soften. The outer world is no longer something to act on and control, it is a place asking us for a relationship. We shift from feeling that we are the rulers of an inanimate universe to recognizing that we are only part of a larger whole. When we are in charge, we act *on;* when we are one of the parts we act *with.* It may be that one of the strongest effects on us of the Stranger's shift is the birth of a new sense of relationship and stewardship with the physical world—and, most likely, with each other. After all, in a synchronicity two things, our inner world and outer events, connect. Connection is a relationship, and in relationship the key words are eros and reciprocity, not power. Perhaps for Western science's power drive the implications of the Stranger's meaning in matter lie in this direction. Only in time will we be sure.

A full understanding of the depths and extent of the Stranger, as another viewpoint on the link between spirit and matter, is at least part of the challenge on which the survival of civilization depends. This seems clear to me from the response of Pauli's dreams to his "big" question. The central role of Pauli's *conscious* work, culminating in the 1927 discovery that won him the Nobel prize and initiated the nuclear age, opened his *unconscious* to the deepest theme of the time, so that his dreams are representative for all of us, prophetic in a sense—reflective of a sensitivity not unlike Nietzsche's. When asked why some people have these "big dreams" and others do not, Jung replied:

As a rule you don't see these things, because most of my patients are not concerned with the welfare of the world. They are much more concerned with their personal welfare, so they produce pictures which have a far more personal significance. Prophetic dreams are rare . . . The true prophecy demands *size* always and not everybody can boast of having that quality.[127]

Pauli was wrestling in that large arena. Fate placed him right on the pulse beat of world events. The war occasioned his extensive questioning and allowed his unconscious to show him and us just how Western science and culture need to grow into the future. Fate led him not only to personal anguish over the guilt of his profession but also to just those people who could have helped him reorient his career. Where Jung was working on the psychoid archetype, Pauli was dreaming of the Stranger and all he represents. The Stranger is plainly a new point of view on life, or, more exactly, an old point of view that is returning to be recast in a modern framework.

We can feel sad that the Stranger's point of view received so little attention in Pauli's life and work, as we can feel sad that Pauli was unable to complete his assignment. His rich account of his unconscious imagery and its concern for the psychological shift that the atomic age is asking now becomes *our* assignment. From Pauli's dreams we can glimpse portraits of those dynamisms that were alive not only in Pauli and his time, but that are also alive within all of us, today. These pressures are still asking us for articulation and response.

In the next chapter I will continue by examining other ways in which the reality symbolized by the Stranger—the fact that intelligent meaning can reside in and arise from matter—has been communicated to us.

---

[127] *Nietzsche's* Zarathustra, vol 1., p. 554.

# 4
# The Transcendental Background

Thus far we have seen the psychoid archetype, the Stranger, Mercurius and the lower trinity as four ways that the unity of spirit and matter has been characterized. There are three other approaches to this. The first has to do with the symbolism of numbers, the second with the dual mandala and the third with the figure of Sophia.

## Dreams and numbers

To continue our discussion, we will ask ourselves another very simple question. Earlier we wondered why there were dreams in the first place, and we found that the answer to the question led to Jung's hypothesis of the archetype, and then eventually to the psychoid archetype. Now another elementary question arises. In the process of understanding dreams, why, when a dream is understood, does the next dream often pick up where the earlier dream left off? Why does a dream which is understood lead to another which, in terms of disclosure, is a step further than the previous one? Recall the example I gave of the woman whose high school love telephoned her. First there were dreams of men attacking her, then the men became a single man, then the man became this fellow and then, in fact, the man telephoned her. At each point when she understood the main idea in a dream, the next dream presented more of what she needed to know to solve her problem. Why is this? Why do dream themes evolve? Why don't they just keep circling around the same point? We know from analytic work that if they *do* circle around the same point it is because they are not understood. As soon as they are understood they move on to discuss the issue one step further. Why?

The answer is initially very simple again: because there is something that makes them do so. There is something "inside" us (but, of course, this "inside" notion is not really accurate) which sees to it that when a dream is understood then the next dream is a step ahead of the previous one. Jung gives this progression a word, and that word is "spirit."

The most concise definition of Jung's use of the word "spirit" is von Franz's description of the term in her book *Number and Time*. There she describes the spirit as "that factor which creates images in the inner field of vision and organizes them into a meaningful order."[128]

In Jung's view this spirit is inborn. There is a capacity that symbolizes what we need to know in the form of an image and which, when that image is understood, symbolizes the next step in the next dream. This capacity "creates images" and then "organizes them into a meaningful order." Whereas the Freudian standpoint holds that the ego makes the unconscious conscious,[129] for Jung there is an "inner" (again, know the inadequacy of that formulation) process which generates images that have the function of making us conscious, and these images evolve over time when they are understood. The goal of therapy in the Jungian view, briefly stated, is to plug into that process, to understand the dreams step-by-step as they advance in their ongoing clarification of what we need to know in order to solve a given impasse or to live forward into a meaningful and creative life.[130]

If that very simple formulation is extended to its fullest

---

[128] *Number and Time*, p. 214.

[129] From Freud's 1933 *New Introductory Lectures on Psychoanalysis*, lecture 21: "Where id was, there shall ego be."—that is, the ego has to rout out the unconscious and take its place bit by bit.

[130] Recall Pauli's dream discussed above from November 24, 1948, where "a gush of air blows the piece of paper" into the blond man's face. The three cultures on which Western civilization is based—the Hebrew, the Greek and the Roman— each have one word for wind and spirit. In Hebrew it is *Ruah* or *Ruach*, in Greek *pneuma* and in Latin *spiritus*. The gust of wind in the dream would thus indicate that the "spirit" is behind the transformation discussed. The transformation is arranged from the depths of Pauli's being.

conclusion, the implications are not so simple after all. The step-by-step evolution of dreams, continuing over the course of a life, forms a built-in principle or direction for the unfolding of life as a whole. If successive dreams move ahead of the previous ones (when that previous one is understood), and if dreams are ongoing throughout our entire life, then the meaningful ordering principle of the spirit must also apply to the unfolding of our life in general. What the spirit "does" from one dream to the next is also what it is doing over the full extent of our life. Again observe why Jungian psychology pays as much attention to the workings of this future-creating spirit in shaping our life as it does to the reactions and adaptations of the ego to past experience. Jungian analysis is interested in far more than the ego, because much of what is actively involved in healing us is this inborn spirit.[131]

The gradient that Jung called the spirit anticipates how we can live forward into a meaningful life. Meaningful living follows the direction revealed by the spirit. We feel life is meaningful when what we do one day develops from what we did the previous day—or, in a larger time frame, when what we are doing one year is a progression of what we did the previous year. Meaning is when we can say, "Well, first I did this and next I did that," or "At first I was involved in such-and-such, but there is a second phase where I

---

[131] A retrospective comment concerning terminology is in order. My dream that prompted this study spoke of a road "between matter and spirit." For the sake of simplicity and clarity I have intentionally skirted around defining the word "spirit" until now. Spirit and matter have been discussed in terms of the nonphysical and the physical, subject and object, inner and outer, psyche and world, etc. That is right, though limited. The spirit, as Jung has defined it from observing the goal-directed quality of dreams, most significantly has to do with life's movement into the future. Originally he thought the spirit was a quality of inner, psychological processes. So equating "spirit" with "subject" or "inside" does not miss the point. But Jung's later reflections on the implications of synchronicity make it clear that the spirit is not solely a psychological phenomenon, since matter, as we have seen, also communicates aspects of the future. So spirit, then, becomes the capacity of the psyche to create forward-looking images—both in our inner, and, synchronistically, in our outer, reality.

have developed and now I am doing such-and-such." The key words here are *first* I did this or experienced this, etc., and *second* I am doing this or am experiencing this. When we feel our life is evolving in some sort of sensible *sequence*, then life is felt to be meaningful.

The words I just used, *first*, *second*, and *sequence*, are counting terms. Number and counting, then, is one of the ways to denote that life is unfolding, and number also, then, is one of the prime representations that dreams utilize to express the progression of life—that is, meaningful living. If our life is going somewhere, there is an order which can be described numerically in the unfolding of the phases of life. There is a one, there is a two, there is a three, a four, a five and so on.[132] Our life, like our dreams, evolves sequentially; if we are living meaningfully; then there is a sequential process within us, and sequence is denoted by counting. In short, *number symbolizes spirit.*

An example of a dream of numbers is in order. A man who had met a possible partner dreamed of seeing this person in an automobile, but the dreamer was unable to read the numbers on the license plate. This suggests that the relationship might be okay as a dalliance, but would not contribute to the meaningful unfolding of the dreamer's life. Indeed, the dreamer had a history of unhappy relationships and the dream of the unreadable license plate numbers proposes that the current fascination is going to be another unhappy liaison. The dreamer was in fact sick of dalliances and so took the hint from the dream and stayed away from the apparent opportunity. Here the dream used numbers as symbols for the spirit, indicating that the person the dreamer had met would not be able to

---

[132] I am aware there is more to be said here, but a fuller discussion would lead too far from our motif. Certainly meaning cannot be understood without reference to history. The link between meaning and history yet awaits investigation in Jungian psychology. The other fact relevant to a discussion of meaning is the *a priori* identity, considered shortly in the sections in this chapter on the dual mandala and on Sophia. Thus, sequence may not be a sufficient condition to establish meaning, but it is surely a necessary one.

be part of the dreamer's life in a meaningful way. The unreadable numbers hints that there would be no unfolding of the dreamer's life in the relationship.

An implication to be drawn from the fact that numbers portray spirit is that there is a numerical structure to the workings of the unconscious. The human being is made such that numerical unfolding gives the sense of a life meaningfully lived. This is just the way we are put together; our personalities come with a built-in numerical set-up. Human processes are not merely random and chaotic. In Jung's view we are constructed with a kind of inner psychological mathematics as a standard feature. We are not simply a bundle of instincts like a collection of wild and unruly horses; a capacity for a long-term, coherent progression of our life is also part of our human heritage: we contain an inborn mathematical structure for growth and meaning.[133]

The psyche is numerically structured, and, we have seen, so is matter. Recall Planck's constant, the whole number ratios of the electron's orbital levels and the overall predictability of radioactive decay.

At the end of his life Jung was impressed with the fact that psyche and matter exhibit mathematical patterns. He thought the link between spirit and matter, between the structuring process of the spirit and the structuring process of matter, was perhaps to be found in number—and in a fuller investigation of the parallels in the numerical structure of spirit and matter. On that basis von Franz wrote her book *Number and Time*, which is an attempt to look at how number appears in dreams and myths as symbols and how

---

[133] This is not to imply that the process is always linear. Although in the long term we can see how life evolves from point A to point B, in the shorter term it sometimes seems that the shortest distance between two major points in our life is a detour. Indeed, a spiral characterizes how the evolution of life can often feel. We might believe we are going around in circles, but in the long run, when we step back from the daily events of life and contemplate our development, we do see we are getting somewhere—in the same way that the movement of a spiral in fact possesses a forward direction.

number appears in the configuration of the material world. By her own account the work is very provisional. It is a first effort to begin unraveling the possible parallels between the makeup of our personality and the structure of the material world. At the end of his life, Jung felt there was a rich harvest awaiting an exploration of the role of numbers in dreams and myths and a comparison of that role with their function in physics and matter. He felt too old to begin yet another field of inquiry and gave some of his first thoughts to von Franz. She continued the work, which culminated in *Number and Time*. She freely confessed that she felt frustrated and uncertain in her attempt:[134]

> I have now written this rather unreadable book, *Number and Time*, making at least a little attempt. . . . I have a feeling one could find out more. . . . I don't know, I'm just groping . . . that's all I can say.[135]

It is important to remember these words when considering her explorations. Her theses will be more instructive if we do not read her as trying to prove anything but rather as trying to begin probing possible connections. Her line of inquiry investigates a completely new perspective on the unity of matter and spirit. Exploring questions concerning domains separated since the birth of the scientific revolution, she does not present polished answers, but instead gives intelligent and thoughtful reflections for our consideration. We are confronted with an attentive approach which asks: Is this something to consider? or Try looking at it this way—what avenue does that open up? or Perhaps if we examined it from this angle . . . I hope that we can bring an equally thoughtful attitude to exploring some of the most salient points of von Franz's book, bringing our own "maternal intellect" to the beauty of her creative undertaking.

---

[134] von Franz, *Psyche and Matter*, pp. 37, 163ff.

[135] Ibid., p. 164.

**Interaction**

The interrelationship between matter and spirit is thus thought to be based on a parallelism of numerical structuring. Because matter and spirit are similarly structured, they are capable of interacting. Summing up this position, von Franz writes:

> Number forms not only an essential aspect of every material manifestation but is just as much a product of the mind (meaning the dynamic aspect of the unconscious psyche).[136]

Her reference to the "dynamic aspect of the unconscious psyche" is what is also called spirit. She goes on:

> Insofar as similar structures manifest themselves through synchronistic phenomena both in the unconscious psyche *and* in matter,[137] the unity of existence (already conjectured by the ancient alchemists) which underlies the duality of psyche and matter becomes more comprehensible to us. Jung applied the term *unus mundus* to this aspect of the unity of existence.[138]

The term *unus mundus* (Latin for one world) is taken from the medieval alchemist Gerhard Dorn.[139] Dorn wrote that once the end state of the alchemical process was reached—that is, after the gold or diamond was produced through the processes carried out by the alchemist in his vessel—there was yet another stage to be completed. That stage consisted of the *lapis* (the end product, or Philosophers' Stone) being united with the world. Then a healing of the world occurred in parallel with the production of the Stone. This final stage Dorn called the *unus mundus*, which expresses the notion of a similarity of structure between the end product of the alchemical process and the outer, physical world. Jung, of course, understood this metaphorically. A synchronicity, as we have seen,

---

[136] Ibid., p. 37.

[137] That is, the same image appears in a dream and in a physical event, or an outer event coincides meaningfully with an inner psychic situation.

[138] Von Franz, *Number and Time,* p. 8.

[139] See *Mysterium Coniunctionis*, CW 14, pars. 759ff.

repeats an inner structure outwardly. In Dorn's *unus mundus* Jung discerned an early attempt to formulate the unity of inner and outer that we find in synchronicity.

Jung writes that the concept of the *unus mundus* is founded "on the assumption that the multiplicity of the empirical world rests on an underlying unity."[140]

The parallel between numerical structures in our personal makeup and those in the material world suggests that there is an underlying unity to life in the deepest sense. The implication of this for psychology is that there is a potential unity to our lives behind, as it were, the vicissitudes of daily living. Also for Dorn, the creation of unity in the *unus mundus* phase of the alchemical process is the re-creation of a unity that existed at the beginning of time. Dorn's statement, again symbolically, suggests that the unity of our life was there at birth, and it is being evidenced, recreated anew, through synchronicities. Hence the touchstone of individuation—to become who you were meant to be, the whole person you originally were.

The same conclusion is reached from a different angle when we consider the implication of Jung's definition of spirit—the process of sequential unfolding within dreams and synchronicity. Our being guided to develop into a whole person or a unitary personality through dreams and synchronicities implies that the person we are becoming was there from the beginning; otherwise, where does the knowledge of who we are meant to be come from? We are forced to conclude that the basic pattern of wholeness that is unfolding was there *in potential* from day one.

Indeed, Jung is not an "existentialist" but rather an "essentialist." The existentialist says that we create ourselves. The essentialist says that we discover ourselves. The existentialist says that "existence precedes essence," which means that we are first born and then we create who we are—our essence—out of the choices that we make. The essentialist position says that "essence precedes

---

[140] Ibid., par. 767; also cited in von Franz, *Number and Time*, p. 9.

existence," which means that we are already born who we are and the process of identity creation is discovering what is already there. For the essentialist past experiences can either hinder or help us in becoming the person we were originally born to be, and in the process of becoming that "inborn" person there is much choice and battle in life to bring our identity into being; the inborn identity is not a free lunch. In the end, however, that creation of who we are is a process of discovery. Perhaps the poet has expressed this with the most eloquence. T.S. Eliot writes in his "Four Quartets:"

> We shall not cease from exploration
> And the end of all our exploring
> Will be to arrive where we started
> And know the place for the first time.[141]

Both Eliot and Jung cast the trials, tribulations and successes of life against a deeper and broader backdrop, ultimately against life's unfolding the mystery of what was there, "where we started."

Concerning the preexistent pattern of who we are, this unity behind our daily life, von Franz observes:

We do know for certain *that the empirical world of appearances is in some way based on a transcendental background.* It is *this* background which, suddenly as it were, falls into our conscious world through synchronistic happenings. [142]

She adds in a footnote to the word "transcendental":

In the sense of "transcending consciousness." I will always use the word "transcendental" in this sense.[143]

The discussion of number symbolism in our inner psychology and outer matter leads to the unity of spirit and matter as a dynamic

---

[141] T.S. Eliot, "Four Quartets," *The Complete Poems and Plays*, p. 145. As an interesting aside: Both Eliot and Jung shared a dear and common friend in the person of Laurens van der Post. See van der Post, *Walk with a White Bushman*, pp. 146ff.

[142] von Franz, *Number and Time*, p. 9.

[143] Ibid., note 9.

principle. Parallel numerical structures are what allow the spirit or image-creating and -ordering factor within us to drop down into matter during a synchronistic moment to convey to us the image of the person we were put here to be. The consideration of number symbolism is an attempt to explain how these two apparently distinct realms can interpenetrate each other, in that "inner" images appear in the events of the material world and in that the "outer" world reflects the images which echo the path to our true and inborn individuality. This is possible because of the shared numerical structure.

Number symbolism explains the unity of matter and spirit from one point of view, and also suggests that the unity—as our *a priori* (prior to experience) identity—is an active presence in our lives. This unity between matter and spirit, the *unus mundus* concept of medieval alchemy, forms one of the basic features of Jungian psychology, a feature that makes Jungian therapeutic work unique among all schools of psychology. For Jung, we are here in potential when we are born, and the reality of this potential is not a mere theoretical curiosity but a dynamic agency inside us *(and outside too!)* ready to drop into the events of daily life through its common structural similarities with the numerical patterns of matter.

Of course, who we potentially are is a mystery until we become that person, which in Jung's view is our essential task in life, facilitated by keeping track of our dreams and synchronistic events.

Having considered number symbolism and its relevance to the relation between spirit and matter as well as to the dynamic force involved in a synchronicity, I will refer to one example of a parallel numerical structure between spirit and matter from von Franz's *Number and Time*. It will be interesting to cast our glance to a specific example of parallel numerical structures, just for a taste of possible practical links. Remember that in looking at the symbolism of numbers in psychology and the role of numbers in matter, von Franz is not trying to prove anything. She is seeking possible parallels in a gesture of inquiry.

Among the examples von Franz studied, comparing numbers in

dreams and myth with numbers in the physical world, the numerical parallel between DNA and the *I Ching* is particularly intriguing. She points out the similarity between the number permutations in the DNA molecule, which is the basis of biological life, and the hexagrams of the *I Ching*, which map the basic portraits of our psychological life. For both DNA and the *I Ching*, the number sixty-four plays a significant organizing role for our potential, whether it be physical or psychological. The same numerical blueprint has an analogous significance in matter and psyche.

Let's start with DNA, our genetic code. DNA is stored in our cells as two strands of molecules twisted around each other to form a double helix. Each strand is made up of just four different kinds of molecules strung together in a long line. DNA provides the instructions that our cells use to build and maintain our body. How does this happen? Think of DNA as a master copy of our genetic code, like a recording from which many copies (RNA) can be made. DNA can be transcribed into RNA to make a working copy of the instructions the cell needs. DNA stays in the nucleus of the cell. The RNA, the copy, goes to other parts of the cell to do its job.

RNA is also a long string of molecules. The four molecules that make up the RNA are called cytosine, guanine, adenine and uracil (designated C, G, A and U for short). RNA is single-stranded with molecules strung together like beads on a string like this:

AUGCACGGUCAAACACGGUGA.

The strand of RNA is read by the machinery in the cell in groups of three like this: AUG, CAC, GGU, CAA, ACA, CGG, UGA. Each grouping is called a codon. These different codons provide the instructions needed by the cell to support and maintain the body.

The key to our discussion is that when the same four kinds of molecules go to make up each of the three molecules in a codon, there are sixty-four possible codons resulting from the variety of these combinations. Our unique genetic predisposition, our genetic fate, is realized in our physical development through the ordering of the sixty-four codons found in our DNA.[144] There are sixty-four building blocks that go to make up the infinite variety of a human being's physical fate. That is DNA.[145]

Now to the *I Ching* and a bit of review. The *I Ching*, as explained earlier, is a Chinese oracle. It goes back to roughly 2000 BC.[146] A reading of the oracle is usually established by asking it about the likely outcome if the questioner takes a particular stand, and the query is generally phrased in this way: "What will be the outcome if I choose to do such-and-such?"[147] Three coins are thrown six times. From the six throws six lines are created, with each line ending up in one of two possible configurations, solid or broken. So a response from the *I Ching* consists of six lines where each line can be one of two types. From the six-line character that is created, the corresponding character in the *I Ching* is consulted, and an answer or commentary is ascertained.

The number of hexagrams that can be created out of six lines, where each line has two possibilities, is sixty-four. Thus there are sixty-four possible responses from the *I Ching* to our questions.[148] Those sixty-four responses represent the possible psychological conditions that characterize life. I've made this simplistic for the sake of the discussion, since my main point here is to look at the mathematical structure of the *I Ching*.[149]

---

[144] The question has been raised whether there being sixty-four codons is really significant in light of the fact that they code for only twenty-one amino acids. In fact, this codon reduncancy does have biological significance and is not mere excess. The point is that the sixty-four possible codons form the "vocabulary" of our genetic code which instructs our physical growth, function and potential.

[145] Thanks to Cynthia Swartz for generously helping me conceptualize the nature of DNA.

[146] Richard Wilhelm and Hellmut Wilhelm, *Understanding the I Ching*, pp. 16f.

[147] We can also ask it for a read on a particularly tense situation, as I noted earlier.

[148] Again, the practical results are more manifold, as the basic responses combine in various permutations, but these are all variations of the sixty-four building blocks or hexagrams of the *I Ching*.

[149] Actually each throw can yield one of four possibilities. But in the *I Ching*

For example, when I was in training in Zürich, I was deliberating whether to isolate myself for a time by renting a small house in the country in order to concentrate on my inner work and studies free of social pressures. I consulted the *I Ching* concerning the likely outcome of this move and threw the three coins six times. The hexagram that was constructed out of those six throws is the Caldron (Figure 18). The caldron refers to a psychological situation characterized by cooking in a pot for the purpose of preparing food. I rented the house and while living there did cook in an intense period of inner examination of difficult emotions and devoted study.

Figure 18. *I Ching* hexagram 50, the Caldron.

What I learned became food for both my soul and my relationships, personal and professional. The *I Ching's* response gave me insight into the viability of my decision to begin a lonely and protracted period of inner self-examination. It also helped me understand the meaning of the difficult moments of living

schema two of those possibilities are actually duplicates, so for the sake of our discussion here we can say that each throw of coins can basically yield one of two possibilities.

there—prepar-ation for my imminent return to the United States.

Sixty-four building blocks go to make up our physical life; sixty-four different characterizations delineate aspects of our psychological fate.

Von Franz points out that these sorts of correspondences—the structure of the substance that creates our physical fate and the structure of what can register our psychological fate—are both based on the same pattern of sixty-four. Here is how she concludes her point:

> This astonishing correspondence seems, more than any other evidence, to substantiate Jung's hypothesis that number regulates both psyche and matter. The same numerical model, a pattern underlying the basic process of human memory and transmission . . . has been discovered, first in China through an introspective examination of the unconscious psyche, and then in the West through genetic research into the living cell.[150]

Analytic work, at the depth Jung envisioned, proceeds with an equal eye to two dimensions. It is crucial for the analyst to be able to see and feel the *a priori* self in the analysand. How does an analyst learn that? By having had the experience of being similarly known in his or her own training; this is why Jungians feel the most important part of analytic training is their own personal analysis. No technique can substitute for knowing from being known. Analysts simply have to be able to discern or intuit whom, in the deepest sense, they are addressing.[151] On the other hand, it is just as crucial for the analyst to be attuned to the details of the analysand's life in time and space, the trials and vicissitudes of daily life. In analysis, then, we slowly try to build a relationship between who the analysand essentially is and how the events of life have

---

[150] *Number and Time*, p. 106.

[151] Jung: "I always let [my patient] see that I was on the side of the [inner] voice, which I recognized as part of his future greater personality, destined to relieve him of his one-sidedness." ("Psychology and Religion," *Psychology and Religion,* CW 11, par. 80

hindered or helped—and are hindering or helping—the development of the real person on the path of individuation, becoming themselves. This does not happen overnight, and in fact can take several years.

Two dimensions, then, press on us in analytic work. As has been stressed, this twofold portrait of life was indispensable to Jung for understanding the nature of the human psyche. Since there was nothing of comparable scope in any other modern theory of behavior available to Jung, he had to look further afield to corroborate his findings. When confronted with what seemed like a new idea Jung would ask himself: Am I the first person who has seen this? Historical analogies were crucial to him in confirming that his observations were not some idiosyncratic whim. He sought historical analogies to corroborate his ideas and to learn from past commentators on the human condition. In this effort he explored ways to extend his understanding of what he observed in his consulting room.

For instance, Jung asked himself where else in Western culture the idea of a singularity within duality could be found. We have seen some of that in the figure of Mercurius, a duality of spirit and matter who belonged as much to the inner world as the outer. There are also two other prime images of the "one in two" that are helpful metaphors. One is the dual mandala, a theme that we find from classical antiquity to the medieval era to modern dreams; the other is the figure of Sophia who likewise takes her root in antiquity, extending quite clearly through the medieval era to the present. I will examine each of these images in turn

**The dual mandala—time and the timeless.**

Jung's research into the symbolism of the mandala is extensive.[152] *Mandala* is Sanskrit for "magic circle." Mandalas are known primarily in Eastern traditions as images used for meditation. They are circular representations of the wholeness of the world (Figures

---

[152] See, in particular, "Concernng Mandala Symbolism," *The Archetypes and the Collective Unconscious*, CW 9i, pars. 627ff.

19-22, next pages). Jung found them present in his own dreams and in those of his patients. He surmised that their role was to convey to the dreamer pictures of his or her individual wholeness.

So dreams use the mandala to indicate the wholeness of the personality—analogous to the way they were understood in religious traditions to indicate the wholeness of the world.[153]

Figure 19. Buddhist mandala.

---

[153] There are of course mandalas in the Christian tradition, and the Native American tradition makes quite vivid use of them in sand paintings.

Figure 20. Notre Dame rose window mandala.

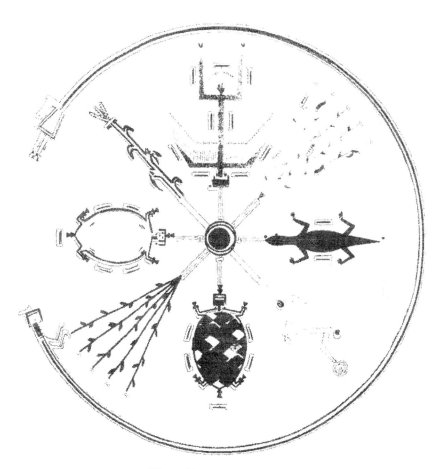

Figure 21. Navajo mandala.

Figure 22. Mandala painted by Jung in 1928.

There is an irony, however, to some of the mandalas that Jung came across. The mandala is said to signify wholeness, unity and indivisibility; yet there are mandala representations of the unity of the world which are dual, which come in pairs. Two mandalas are required to make up the oneness of life in some instances. It will be no surprise to see that very often the two mandalas embody just the two aspects of life, the timeless plan as well as the time-bound part of daily living, that we are reflecting on here. The timeless mandala is thought to be the portrait of a transcendental background, in other words symbolic of an ordering principle to life that is not directly observable as a datum of experience that can be measured, but which can nevertheless be inferred as the larger direction of life is felt. It is this transcendent pattern that has an effect on the world of time and space portrayed by the second mandala.

Perhaps the dual mandala closest to our experience is the astrological chart. Whether or not you believe in astrology is not the point. The point is how humanity has felt a need to exemplify the experience that life is made up of two levels. Astrology presupposes two dimensions: there is the immutable world of the planets, which portrays the larger pattern of life evident at the time of our birth, and then there is our own individual version of the relationship between the arrangements of the planets at various times of our life. Astrology attempts to build a bridge between the larger pattern in the cosmos and events on the earth. Events on earth are always referenced to another, heavenly pattern.[154]

Another dual mandala, one that we find discussed by von Franz in *Number and Time*, is described in Plato's *Timaeus*. Von Franz:

> There Plato assumes the existence of an external extracosmic realm in which ideal geometric solid forms, latent within themselves, timelessly coexist. Since the Creator of the universe could not transfer all these figures *simultaneously* into his cosmic creation, he decided to create a moving age of the external unity and its timeless co-

---

[154] For an authoritative exposition of the correspondence between astrology and Jungian psychology, see Alice O. Howell, *The Heavens Declare:Astrological Ages and the Evolution of Consciousness.*

existent order.... In this way time came into being and formed a bridge between the two models, one of which was a timeless continuum, and the other a rotating, and as such, time-bound mandala.[155]

[This early attempt] to draw up a cosmic mandala already demo n-strates that it was thought to exist beyond material space and time, or entirely corporally, or within cosmic matter in a separate, distinct form. In Plato's work this problem led to the construction of a double cosmic mandala, one aspect of which was considered to be timeless and non-material, and the other to be cyclically moving in space and time.[156]

Thus in early antiquity we find the need to conceive of life in terms of two systems that somehow intersect or otherwise express the fact that the unity of life is made up of two parts. And these two parts, typically symbolized by a circle representing a higher, transcendent ordering background on the one hand and by the circular shape of the earth on the other hand, make up the unity of life.

The most dramatic example of the dual mandala considered in Jung's work relates to a dream Pauli had when he sought help after the collapse of his first marriage. To make sense of the dream, Jung discusses a medieval parallel to it. We will do well first to consider that and then to look at Pauli's dream. The text Jung mentions comes from a fourteenth century Norman poet, Guillaume de Digullerville, prior of a monastery of Châlis, and concerns a vision of paradise. Jung describes the vision:

Paradise consists of forty-nine rotating spheres. They are called "siècles," centuries, being prototypes or archetypes of the earthly centuries. But, as the angel who serves as a guide to Guillaume explains . . . [they are in] eternity and not ordinary time. A golden heaven surrounds all the spheres. When Guillaume looked up to the golden heaven he suddenly became aware of a small circle, only three feet wide and of the colour of sapphire. He says of this circle:

---

[155] von Franz, *Number and Time*, p. 178.

[156] Ibid.

"It came out of the golden heaven at one point and reentered it at another, and it made the whole tour of the golden heaven." Evidently the blue circle was rolling like a disc upon a great circle which intersected the golden sphere in heaven

Here, then, we have two different systems, the one golden, the other blue, and the one cutting through the other. What is the blue circle?[157]

The angel explains that the blue circle is the calendar year, which shows the ecclesiastical days of the Church. Jung comments: "The blue circle is the ecclesiastical calendar. So here we have . . . the element of time."[158]

Note in particular how the universe is made up of two main circles: the timeless, transcendent heavens and the time-defined calendar of the Church. A larger system of the heavens intersects, and is intersected by, the events on earth, that is, the days of the year as typified by the Church calendar.

Pauli's dream from the early 1930s is as follows:

There is a vertical and a horizontal circle, having a common centre. This is the world clock. It is supported by the black bird (Figure 23, next page).

The vertical circle is a blue disc with a white border divided into 4 x 8 = 32 partitions. A pointer rotates upon it.

The horizontal circle consists of four colours. On it stand four little men with pendulums, and round about it is laid the ring that was once dark and is now golden (formerly carried by four children).

The world clock has three rhythms or pulses:

1. The small pulse: the pointer on the blue vertical disc advances by 1/32.

2. The middle pulse: one complete revolution of the pointer.

---

[157] "Psychology and Religion," *Psychology and Religion*, CW 11, pars. 116ff.

[158] Ibid., par. 118.

At the same time the horizontal circle advances by 1/32.

3. The great pulse: 32 middle pulses are equal to one complete rotation of the golden ring.[159]

Figure 23. Artist's conception of Pauli's world clock.

---

[159] Ibid., par. 111.

Interestingly enough, Marie-Louise von Franz also speaks of double mandalas/wheels, referring to two orders of time as "two incompatible systems that cannot be put together but are complementary."[160] (Figure 24).

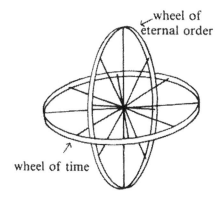

Figure 24. Double mandalas: two sorts of time.

Pauli's dream emphasizes a horizontal and a vertical circle. The horizontal circle alludes to a ring that was "formerly carried by four children." These children carrying the ring had appeared in previous dreams from this time period. They epitomized Pauli's emotional conflict and acute suffering after his divorce and during the years of his personal crisis.[161] The horizontal circle thus represents the dimension of time and space, and Pauli's suffering in it.

The vertical clock face is blue. Jung interprets the blue color as an emphasis on the vertical, spanning blue sky to blue ocean.[162] So the vertical part of the clock represents the heavenly or transcen-

---

[160] *On Divination and Synchronicty: The Psychology of Meaningful Chance,* p. 108. She had previously commentted: "As far as I can see, there is everywhere this idea of two orders . . . acausal orderedness on the one hand, which is timeless, and synchronistic events, which enter linear time, on the other side." (Ibid., p. 107)

[161] "Individual Dream Symbolism in Relation to Alchemy," *Psychology and Alchemy,* CW 12, pars. 272f., 301f., 307f.

[162] Ibid., par. 320.

dental background of timeless possibility which descends to the earth, crossing time and space and seeking realization there.

Why would Pauli have such a dream? Most likely because he did not want to accept that life is made up of two such dimensions. The dream was trying to show Pauli, who at the time was a rational physicist, a materialist and a cynic, that he could not understand life without accepting its complexity. It is being suggested—by the horizontal circle and its association with previous dream images referring to his emotional pain—that he look very closely at the events in his life in time and space and take responsibility for his role in them. This is what ego development is about—observing behavior and taking responsibility for it. Thus it is very important that we pay meticulous attention to the events and patterns of daily life. But reality is not the whole story. The other dimension that Pauli is being shown, in the image of the vertical circle, is his fundamental, *a priori* identity, the inborn story of his life. The purpose of his crisis in the 1930s was to bring his attention to this fact, to recognize who he, at essence, was to be, and to bring that identity into time and space, that is, to make sure his vertical circle intersected with his horizontal one. What Pauli would have found repugnant at the time was that the blue color of the vertical circle linked it to the color of the heavens, attesting to the spirituality of the vertical circle's meaning—conceived in the way Jung recognized "spirit."[163]

As the medieval vision of Guillaume de Digullerville shows, and as the vision of a modern physicist attests, the dual mandala is a living image which portrays that a single life is made up of two parts, the here-and-now and something else. This something else is the greater pattern for our life, and its intent is to enter matter as we take the steps to become the person we were born to be.

---

[163] Jung was interested in the phenomenology of the spirit, that is, how it works and appears to us, not whether it has any metaphysical reality. He believed that the latter was the business of theologians. Each religious tradition sees the phenomenology of the spirit wrapped up in its own dogmatic assumptions. Jung was interested simply in the existence of the spirit and how it functions in human growth.

Pauli's dream and its historical precedent clearly demonstrate the dual mandala image. Often dreams are more subtle. They do not come with a "look here for dual mandala" note attached. The theme is not infrequently hidden within apparently mundane allusions. Seeing the link between the dual mandala and this timeless or spirit dimension usually requires some effort.

In the following dream; the dual mandala pattern is not obvious at first, but it does become clear upon close reflection.

The dreamer was a woman about forty. She was unhappy in a corporate job. It was a financially lucrative position with many perks, but the atmosphere was cut-throat and the people who ran the business did not inspire her respect. When she became involved in an affair with a man in the same industry, she saw even more of the ruthless and soul-killing underbelly of her business. She became more and more discouraged, eventually quitting her job. She went back to school to obtain a graduate degree in a field that interested her and from there pursued a new career. Although there were no dramatic synchronicities during this process, the affair was itself a kind of synchronicity. Just the right creepy man was there to give her the final lesson in what she knew subliminally—that this field and its big egos were not what she really wanted.

Without doubt her collision with the material world instigated by her erotic desire brought on a fundamental reorientation in her life. She began to reconsider everything about it and eventually started down the path of a new career which she felt was based in who she was. Parallel to the career change was a divorce from a very unsatisfying marriage and her taking up a happier relationship in which she was treated with kindness and love.

During her period of transition she had the following dream. A summary of its first part will be followed by a verbatim account of the end of the dream, which relates to the dual mandala image.

She is in southern California, in Hollywood. She is sitting in an expensive home, and a woman is there who is a decorative artist—not a true artist, a decorative artist. Next in the dream she walks out into the street. It is warm, but she is covered from head to toe in clothing.

> She goes to a restaurant where her co-workers are sitting and they don't leave a seat for her and they don't invite her to sit with them. She leaves, and she feels sad.

Now I quote from her text:

> Then I am on another planet. It is very dark. Tom Cruise is there. A voice of some authority is telling him that his wife as she always was is with him, and their daughter is to work with fire. It was written long ago.[164]
> Then I see him in the distance boarding a plane with his wife. She looks like the singer Avril Lavigne, and she is wearing wings like an angel.

Before we look at the last paragraph, some comments on the first part of the dream will provide the context for the ending.

The Southern California and Hollywood setting refers to the superficiality and glitter that went along with her profession, which was something like a slick marketing job. Although the people she associated with professionally were in fact sure they were the hip and cultural elite of the city, the dream portrays that type of person as a merely decorative artist—not a real artist but a tinseled one. What passed for creativity in the self-congratulatory society where she worked was really just decorative tripe, the dream tells her, and the decorative artist is also what she, the dreamer, was in danger of turning into. Her affair, the heartache and the realizations gained during her analytic work were what kept her from turning into this cliché herself.

She is bundled up in sunny southern California, and this equates to her protection against the chilly atmosphere around her. Even though the temperature may have been warm in her trendy world, the hearts in it were not; actually it was a brutally cold environment. She leaves that house and also sees that there is no room for

---

[164] Jung also has discussed this fact as our "ground-plan" which is established before birth. (See L. Frey and R. Schärf, eds., *The Psychological Interpretation of Children's Dreams: Notes on Lectures Given by Prof. Dr. C.G. Jung at the Eidgenosische Technische Hochschule*, p. 18; also *Aion*, CW 9ii, par. 297.)

her in the restaurant. That corresponds to her becoming sick of the kind of professional ethos she was in and leaving it. This first part of the dream is introductory.

The next part, quoted directly, shows her turning inward to find out who she is and to make a change in her life. That inner questioning is symbolized by the second planet, which introduces the dual mandala into the dream. The trip to the second planet is her journey to the second circle of the dual mandala where the true story of her identity was written. There she finds a woman as she always was and a story that was written long ago. Although the dual mandala theme rather sneaks up in the image of the two planets, the *a priori* nature of her identity could hardly be stated more forcefully. Her identity really is something that always was and that was written long ago.

Jung's work strives to be true to this question: Who have I been *meant* to be from day one, and what do I have to go through to become that? A simple-minded therapeutic approach with her would have been to discuss what drew her into an unsatisfying and painful affair, another situation, like her marriage, where she ended up unhappy. By following instead the purpose of the events in her life—that there was a purpose is indicted by the symbolism of the dual mandala in the dream—she was able to journey into the knowledge of the mystery of her life, to see who she was really meant to be and to take the steps to put her true identity into time and space.

The dreamer's association to Tom Cruise was the film *Mission: Impossible.* Thus he represents the dreamer's heroic strength that got her up to this planet and that will bring her back to earth. She had the strength to leave the previously familiar world of time and space and to begin inquiring into who she truly was. After she had that realization,the dream goes on to indicate that she would also have the strength to come down to earth and put it into action. The work with fire stands for the emotions she was dealing with in her affair and in the process of self-inquiry, as well as starting over in life at the age of forty-something. As Jung has said, "Consciousness takes its origin in passion."[165]

The dream shows a practical example of the two dimensions of life, the consideration of which Jung felt paramount to analytic work. The dream's text indicates very beautifully the dual aspect of true living: the fire, turmoil and strength that it takes to pull off a relationship to both time and space and to the true story of our life. I especially appreciate the way Laurens van der Post has referred to this "true story of our life" in one of his descriptions of Jung:

> He went on, in that deep bass voice of his to tell me at great length, how his work as a healer did not take wing—the metaphor is mine—until he realized that the key to the human personality was its story. Every human being at core, he held, had a unique story and no man could discover his greatest meaning unless he lived and, as it were, grew his own story. Should he lose his story or fail to live it, he lost his meaning, became disoriented, the collective fodder of tyrants and despots, or ended up, as so many did, alienated and out of their own minds, as had the patients in the Burghölzli Asylum to whom he owed this insight.[166]

In Jung's treatment of the story "written long ago" in Pauli's dream, symbolized by the vertical clock, he paid particular attention to the vertical clock's blue color. Jung cites another amplification of the blue color of that circle: the blue of the Virgin Mary's robe.[167] The vertical circle therefore can be seen to possess a feminine quality. An additional feminine reference is also implicit in Pauli's indicating that there were thirty-two (4 x 8 = 32) segments of the vertical clock. In commenting on this aspect of the dream Jung interpreted the number thirty-two as a reference to Wisdom;[168] in other words, to Sophia. Twice in the characteristics of the vertical clock, its blue color and its thirty-two segments, we find an allusion

---

[165] *Visions: Notes of the Seminar*, vol. 1, p. 409.

[166] Van der Post and Jane Taylor, *Testament to the Bushman*, p. 138.

[167] "Individual Dream Symbolism in Relation to Alchemy," *Psychology and Alchemy*, CW 12, par. 320.

[168] Ibid., par. 313.

to the feminine, in particular to the figure of Sophia. So now it will be appropriate for our discussion to turn to her, the feminine representation of two dimensions.

## Sophia

In our civilization Sophia makes her first appearance in ancient Greek philosophy, roughly between 600 and 300 BCE.[169] In Greek, Sophia means wisdom, so *philosophia,* the etymological Latin root of philosophy, means the love of wisdom.

Sophia next appears in the Hebrew Scriptures, in Proverbs 8, tentatively dated to 400 BCE:

> I, Wisdom, dwell with experience and judicious knowledge. Mine are counsel and advice. Mine is strength, understanding. By me kings reign and lawgivers establish justice. By me princes govern and nobles, all the rulers of the earth. Those who love me I also love, and those who seek me find me. With me are riches and honor. My fruit is better than gold. On the way of duty I walk, along the paths of justice. The Lord begot me, the first-born of his ways, the forerunner of his prodigies of long ago. From of old I was poured forth. When there were no depths I was brought forth, when there were no foundations or springs of water, before the mountains were settled into place. When he established the heavens I was there, when he made firm the skies above, when he fixed fast the foundations of the earth; when he set for the sea its limit so that the waters should not transgress his command; then I was beside him as his craftsman. I was his delight, day by day, playing before him all the while, playing on the surface of his earth; and I found delight in the sons of men.[170]

This is a portrait of God that we did not hear much about in Sunday school—that God has a female partner whose presence preceded the creation of the world. As this Biblical image gave rise to tradition, Sophia, "first born of his ways," was eventually thought to personify the plan of creation by which God fashioned the

---

[169] The historical discussion of Sophia is taken from Edward F. Edinger, *Transformation of the God Image,* pp. 53ff.

[170] Proverbs 8:21-31; New American Bible (condensed); cited in ibid., pp. 53f.

world.[171] Her reference to "I was there" when the entire firmament was formed was taken to mean that she was the blueprint for what God would create.

After her appearance in the Hebrew tradition, Sophia surfaces next in Gnosticism. This is a term applied to a whole range of sects whose basic theology has certain tenets in common. Most likely the Gnostic view can be traced back earlier than Christianity, but it is the emergence of Gnosticism in early Christianity, probably in 100 to 300 AD, that concerns our discussion.

The supposition common to Gnostic interpretations is that when God created the world, pieces of God got stuck in the material world just created, thus there are little sparks of God trapped in everything. The variations on that story are endless, but the basic theme is consistent across the range of Gnostic groups. At the birth of Christianity there were competing interpretations concerning what had just happened during the life of Christ and how the Scriptures were to be interpreted. The Gnostics were those espousing an understanding of Christianity characterized by a theology of God caught in matter. The coalescing Church eventually declared this interpretation a heresy, and Gnostic tenets all but disappeared from Christianity.[172]

In some of the Gnostic versions it was Sophia, the feminine aspect of God, who became trapped in matter. Other accounts held that it was God Himself, or some lesser part of God (there were hierarchies of God in the Gnostic view) who was caught in the world at creation, but some held that God had a female consort, and it was this consort, Sophia, who had been snatched up by matter. In any case, the Gnostic idea of redemption was that the faithful should live so that the part of God or Sophia which was caught in them would return to God at their death. It was God who needed to be redeemed, made whole again, by religious observation, so the

---

[171] See Marie-Louise von Franz, *Aurora Consurgens: A document attributed to Thomas Aquinas on the problem of opposites in alchemy,* pp. 155f.

[172] For a more compehensive discussion, see Edward F. Ednger, *The Psyche in Antiquity, Book 2: Gnosticism and Early Christianity.*

practical ethics of Gnostic living derived from the Gnostic sense of the redemption of God. For our purposes the key point is that Gnosticism considered Sophia as the part of God trapped in matter.

Two major traditions converge on the psychological image of Sophia: the Hebrew and the Gnostic. From the Hebrew we find that Sophia is the plan of creation by which the world was created. From the Gnostic we find that Sophia is trapped in the material world. Both of these commentaries make up the psychology of Sophia when she appears in our dreams. On the one hand Sophia is a plan for creation and on the other hand she is an experience to be found at the heart of matter.

If we interpret these observations psychologically, we reach a conclusion fed by two streams. First, Sophia, as the plan of creation, represents the plan of *our* creation, the pre-existent plan of our life. Second, insofar as she is caught in matter, Sophia signifies those experiences where the plan of our life, our *a priori* identity, comes to us though our dealings with occurrences in the physical world, in concrete reality. Sophia is a picture of those experiences in and from the material world which convey to us, through their embodying symbolic reality, images of our true and genuine selfhood, our unique story—"as it always was"—waiting to be lived in time and space.

A beautifully simple, though hardly simplistic, dream suggests these two aspects of Sophia. The dreamer was a professional woman who had just finished graduate school and was in the process of a career change. She was, by nature, a genuinely religious person, not in any conventional, going-to-church sort of way, but she longed for "right work," as the Buddhists say, for a way both to earn a living with integrity and to feel that, in doing the work, she was living in tune with the will of God. During the time that she was reexamining her values and her wish to achieve something substantial in life, a time not without storms of depression, uncertainty and doubt, she dreamed:

> I see a sketched circle in pencil. My job is to study that sketch in black and white. Next to it are mounds of colored clay. I am to study

that circle and recreate the two-dimensional circle in three-dimensional reality and in color with clay.

The sketched circle (mandala!) in pencil would be the *a priori* outline of her life, her selfhood in potential, corresponding to the story "written long ago" which we saw previously. It is there in her, but only as a sketch. Her job in the dream is twofold, to study that sketch in order to know who she is, and to recreate the two-dimensional, theoretical plan of her life in three-dimensional reality. Both the preexistent pattern and the concrete reality of three-dimensional color are emphasized in the dream. The recreation of the black and white figure can only be accomplished if she gets her hands dirty with the earthen clay, and the resultant circle must be in color, that is, involve her emotional participation. Her concrete life in time and space must be of one circular piece—whole, not fragmented and not piecemeal, a physically real accomplishment. She is to construct, in time and space and in the fullness of her emotional commitment, who she has already been sketched to be. The two aspects of Sophia, the plan before creation and the presence of that plan in matter, are both allusions in the dream. The dreamer was encouraged and felt that her struggles were worth the pain.

Although the dream above does not directly touch on synchronicity, the following comments on a dream, cited by Edward F. Edinger, does show the connection between the guidance of physical events and the plan before creation:

> It was as though I was experiencing the dream on two levels simultaneously. On the one hand it was unique, spontaneous, and unrehearsed. On the other hand I seemed also to be playing a role and re-enacting a *story* I had once known but forgotten. The levels were inextricably connected. I was playing the role perfectly just because I was really living it at the same time. I made up my lines as I went along but I seemed to be helped by the fact that I had once known the story. When each situation came up it struck some chord of memory

which came to my assistance.[173]

The dream shows that, as we set about investigating the story we once knew, Sophia—as the plan of creation—responds, and certain situations in life come to our assistance. Synchronistic events arise to help direct our way, giving our two-dimensional potential its three-dimensional possibilities for understanding who we are, where we are going and what we are to create in time and space for ourselves, our family and our community.

Of course, Sophia was not about to leave Pauli alone either.[174] In November of 1953, about five years before his death, Pauli dreamt:

A Chinese woman (elevated to the rank of a "Sophia") is present with two men, one of whom is the Master.[175] I am the fourth. She says to me: "You must allow us to play every conceivable combination of chess." In a subsequent half-waking fantasy she announces, in a numinous voice: "In your drawings one element is perfectly correct and another transitory and false. It is correct that the lines number six, but it is false to draw six points. See here—," and I saw:

Figure 25. Pauli's square and diagonals in dream.

—a square with clearly marked off diagonals [Figure 25]. [She says:] "Can you see now finally the four and the six? Four spatial points and six lines or six pairs out of four points. They are the same lines that exist in the *I Ching*. There the six, containing three as a latent factor, are correct. Now observe the square more closely: four of the lines are of equal length, the other two are longer—they are 'irration-

---

[173] Edinger, *Ego and Archetype*, p. 119.

[174] The "very beautifully bright woman" in the Peter Strom dream (above, p. 112) was probably a preview of Sophia.

[175] A later name Pauli gave to the Stranger.

ally related.' There is *no* figure with four points and six equal lines. *For this reason symmetry cannot be statically produced and a dance results.* The *coniunctio* refers to the exchange of places during this dance. One can speak of a game or rhythms and rotations. *Therefore the three, already contained in a latent form in the square, must be dynamically expressed.*"[176]

To round out the considerations of this chapter, I will limit my commentary on the dream to mentioning those details that will refine our appreciation of Sophia.

Sophia invites Pauli to a game of chess. Chess is reported to have originated in India where it was said to be an earthly mirror image of the stars' battle in heaven. A game of chess was the earthly reflection of a drama among the stars in the heavens. The game represented the pattern from which a person's destiny proceeds as it was shaped by the drama of the stars.[177] Immediately we can see here the link to the unity of spirit and matter. If Pauli is being invited to play a game of chess with Sophia, then once again we glimpse the challenge to examine life from two perspectives—from the heavenly pattern and from the events on earth which are shaped by that pattern, and how those events can convey the pattern of our larger story residing in a realm beyond earthly time and space.[178] The rest of the dream attempts to persuade Pauli that a receptivity to that transcendental plan of Sophia, and an openness to reevaluating attitudes and plans on the basis of Sophia's presence in matter, is a dynamic, not a static, process. Sophia's presence in our life requires the flexibility to perceive and express what she suggests. A dynamic process cannot be communicated to a static person.

The game of chess in the dream brings up an associated image

---

[176] Von Franz, *Number and Time*, p. 108 (slightly modified); van Erkelens, *Wolfgang Pauli*, p. 185 (dream 35).

[177] Von Franz, *Number and Time*, p. 296.

[178] That Chinese characteristics were attributed to Sophia in Pauli's dream is no surprise: "The idea that meaning lies concealed in events themselves was, as Richard Wilhelm has shown, predominant in earliest Chinese culture." (Ibid., pp. 200f.)

that is one of the most frequent symbols of Sophia in our unconscious—stars. Stars exist in patterns, so a constellation of stars is a very apt portrayal of Sophia as the pattern of our life. The fact that stars seem to be embedded in the night sky likewise evokes Sophia in her sense of being scattered throughout the universe, caught there since the first day of creation. Since stars, patterns of stars and starlight are such frequent images of the domain of Sophia, a dream of starlight will give us another idea of how Sophia appears in the language of the unconscious.

This is the dream of a young man who was cruelly betrayed. The recognition of his naiveté in not seeing the real character of the betrayer until it was too late set him on a new path of belief in his creative powers. In that sense he came to see the heartache as purposive, and it did in fact stimulate his considerable creative prowess in a new direction. During the time he was turning back to himself and examining whence his life had come and where it was going, he dreamed:

> It is night. I'm in a rural area which is extremely dark—no city lights. I look up at the sky and see that the stars are particularly bright, exceptionally clear. I have never been in a place this dark and have never been able to see the stars so plainly. I can make out the definiteness of the constellations in a way that I had not noticed before. I observe their different patterns which are very pronounced and almost seem to be in the stars themselves. No wonder ancients saw images in the heavens. The brilliance of the starry night sky with its forms is magnificent.

The patterns in the stars, another image of Sophia, are visible because the dreamer was in despair and consumed with heartache, the darkness in the dream. The reflection on the dreamer's course of life that was signified by the dream came at the instigation of a crisis in the outer world. The dreamer came to see that the event itself was a symbol, offered at Sophia's bidding, to put him on the right track of his creative life, the pattern of his life that was, in fact, written in his stars.

The experience of Sophia is not always a picnic. She captures the darkness and struggle that are sometimes the price of hearing our real story. It is amazing what kinds of experiences we are induced to consider if we really want to recognize the extent of the human capacity to heal psychologically and to find our inborn story. Sophia sometimes charges a high price but her offerings are likewise of singular value.

The discussion of Sophia here has touched on historical traditions that have shaped her character. In the next chapter I place Jung's work—and the range of considerations on matter and spirit that he has presented—in their wider historical context, this time against the backdrop of Western cultural evolution. Through such a perspective we will have a better grasp of where we stand in light of the challenges that the unity of matter and spirit put to our way of thinking and living.

We are all pilgrims in our longing and search for the timeless (figure 26).

Figure 26. The hole open to eternity—
the spiritual pilgrim discovers another world.

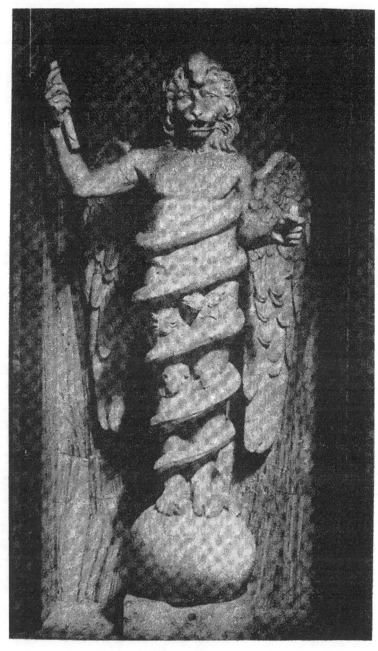

Figure 27. The Mithraic god *Aion* (Roman, ca. 300 AD).

# 5
# Jung's Spiritual Testament

## *Aion*

Jung's *Aion* is his most comprehensive exposition of Western history. The title of the book is taken from the Mithraic god of the same name (Figure 27). Mithraism, one of the religions popular during Roman times, was a particular favorite of the Roman legions. Aion was a god of long duration in Mithraism; his name is the etymological root of our word eon. No doubt Jung chose the title to suggest his main thesis in *Aion*, namely that Western history is made up of several long-term phases. Stated simply, it is Jung's position throughout the book that up to the present time there have been two major one-thousand-year phases to the two-thousand-year expanse of Western civilization.

The first thousand-year epoch began with the birth of Christianity, following the decadence of late antiquity.[179] The psychological situation of the Roman era was characterized by an atmosphere of despair. Hedonism, brutality and an unchecked power drive were rampant. No civilization, no human society, no enterprise of corporate living can survive under these circumstances; it will simply burn itself up in valueless intensity. Unbridled instinct was in the process of destroying the very fabric of civilized life in Rome.

The great psychological accomplishment of Christianity, in contrast, is that it put an end to Roman barbarism. At a time when violence and greed—political, social and personal—triumphed in daily life, Christianity offered an entirely different set of values: the non-material versus the material, the spirit versus the flesh, self-abnegation versus hedonism, selfless love versus egotistical power,

---

[179] This is not to grant favor to Christianity above other world religions; it is just to observe the political and social effect of Christendom on Western civilization.

surrender versus domination, poverty versus wealth, and so on. Against the material excesses of the Romans, Christianity was born as an ethical, nonworldly, spiritual movement in sharp contrast to the dissolute gluttony of Rome and her colonies.

Jung saw history moving in pendulum swings.[180] Of course matter and spirit are essentially united within human nature; these two realms belong together and are two sides of a whole. But the way they have manifested throughout our civilization is as separate poles. At the end of antiquity, the pendulum of history had swung far in the direction of greed. As a reaction from within human nature, another swing began out of the Christian experience; to save civilization from emotional incineration and to bring stability to the social order the pendulum went toward a temperate spirit. The material world was everything in antiquity, and this manifested as desire for sexual experience, power and acquisition. Spirit, that inborn ordering factor, then emerged in Christianity as a longing for separateness from the world. That spirit aspired to evolve meaningfully and with stability, and to discern a greater pattern within the travail of living. At the birth of the Christian era values based in the material world were in charge, but with the rise of Christianity values of the spirit took their place.

The historical movement from matter to spirit reached its apogee in the Gothic cathedrals of Europe, where we can see the impulse to move up into spiritual realms, as Christianity understood them. Up, away from the earth, to the higher point of view of the spirit, is what the Gothic was all about. The spirit, so clearly reflected in Gothic architecture, seeks vertical movement, strengthening reason, countering the pull of matter.

As the vertical, spiritual movement was ending, another swing back to the material world was starting. This movement back toward matter is apparent in the Renaissance, where nature, the body, and indeed history, once more attracted human attention.

---

[180] He associated this with the phenomenon of *enantiodromia,* a term which means that any extreme eventually changes into its opposite.

While Christianity had emphasized an austere spirit and the vertical dimension of life, for a second time Western culture became interested in the affairs of earthly matter—as far as the eye could see, to the horizon and beyond. The pendulum had swung back to matter, and this could be seen in the age of exploration, as new horizons beckoned. The scientific revolution resulted from a renewed interest in things of the earth.

In the first thousand-year phase of Western history, characterized by the spirit, people looked up to the heavens for guidance. In the second thousand-year phase, characterized by matter, people looked out over the material world for their orientation and adventure. There was, of course, a period of overlap as the purely spiritual Christian phase dwindled and the modern worldly imperialistic and scientific one gathered momentum.

Jung's view of the West's two eons brings us to today. In his view, the psychological task of our time is to realize the unity of spirit and matter—the vertical spiritual and the horizontal material—and thus to mitigate the age-long pendulum swings. The materialism of imperialism and science, expressions of the swing to horizontal values, has run its course as manipulating the physical world becomes less satisfying to the living human heart and down-right dangerous to our existence. Jung felt that our challenge is to let the world be the place where, in acknowledging our desires, we can again find the guidance of the spirit. We are fascinated by the material world: this much is clear. But neither overcoming worldly fascination and desire (the Christian pendulum swing of the past) nor being consumed by them (the secular swing) is to be our path now. Our challenge is to experience *and* reflect on desire, finding the guiding spirit within it as did the woman who traveled to another planet in her dream. The next phase of Western history is to be characterized by a synthesis, where equilibrium is found.

The creation of unity between matter and spirit was not just an interesting puzzle for Jung. His appreciation for the importance of synthesis is a fruit of his understanding of history. Jung articulated this view of human nature because he felt that our moment in history is asking this of us. Jung's approach—his theoretical understanding of psychology and his practical application of this grasp in a day-to-day way in the consulting room—is a reflection of how he recognizes the psychological tenor of our time.

We are living in a period in which swings of history are making specific demands. Jung's psychology is, certainly, interested in helping us grow from and out of our psychological maladies; but it is, at core, also aimed at helping us grow from and out of those maladies in a way that is a response to what history requires, which is that we turn to the unity of matter and spirit and begin to live it in our daily lives. We should neither spiritualize nor materialize, but seek the center where spirit and matter have their common root. And Jung did his best to present the point of view that will help this become a reality: recognition of the limits of causality in explaining behavior, acknowledgment of the purpose and arc of experience, a recognition of the work of the unconscious in symbolizing the same, and a recognition of new formulations linking matter and spirit such as number and related images.

There was a historical purpose behind Jung's discoveries, and we have seen how features of his view surfaced in the separate but strangely related theory of quantum physics. The pressure of history is why the fresh paradigm appeared in two such diverse disciplines during one of the darkest periods of Western history—in the wake of Europe's collapse after the First World War and as Europe prepared for another monumental bloodbath. History is telling us we are in need of a fresh point of view.

### *Aurora Consurgens*

Another place where these historical shifts appear, just as Jung discussed them, is in a series of medieval visions called *Aurora Consurgens* (Latin, "Rising Dawn"). In this medieval text the psychological tenor of each age is symbolized by a different kind of light.

As the pendulum was in the process of reversing from spirit back to matter, in the thirteenth century a cleric had a remarkable series of visions. It is supposed that this cleric was Thomas Aquinas and that the visions occurred to him on his deathbed.[181] Whether or not it was really Aquinas who had these visions is not important for our purposes, because whoever it was would have been someone like him, an epitome of the otherworldly and spiritual Christian values that would be coming under assault from the counterstream soon to be surfacing in the Renaissance. Even though, or perhaps more accurately just because, the cleric was a devout Christian in the medieval sense, the dynamics of history that would break on the scene were activated in his unconscious. He was a paradigm of the one-sided spirit. Thus it is not hard to understand that the swing that would appear next in history was occurring in his psychology to bring the specifically Christian view in himself back from its lofty height—as it would also occur more generally on the world stage to bring Western civilization back from one-sided spirituality.

Marie-Louise von Franz's interpretation of the visions in *Aurora Consurgens* provides a moving commentary pertinent to our look at the pendulum of history.

The visions start with images of blackness, disorientation and flood, indicating that the individual having the visions has lost his grip on daily life and the previous system of orientation that sustained him—the Christian orientation—was being eclipsed in a mood of despair and darkness. So the first vision is an image of the collapse of Christian effectiveness. A subsequent principal image then stands at the center of the series. The visionary is speaking of Wisdom's house and of her generosity:

> Wisdom hath built herself a house, which if any man enter in he shall be saved . . . . O how blessed are they that dwell in this house; for therein everyone that asketh receiveth . . . . To them that unlock this house shall be befitting holiness and also length of days . . . so that face to face and eye to eye, they shall look upon all the brightness of the sun and moon.[182]

---

[181] Von Franz, ed., *Aurora Consurgens*, pp. 405ff.

[182] Ibid., pp. 314ff.

The treasure house to be entered into is the house of Wisdom, in other words the house of Sophia. She is the centerpiece, suggesting that the ascent of Sophia will be an aspect of what follows the darkness of the collapse of trust in Christendom.[183] Von Franz points out that the phrase "face to face and eye to eye" is a reference to I Corinthians 2:9, where the passage states that what is seen is "what things God has prepared for those who love him." Von Franz continues:

> In our text, significantly enough, it is not actually God that is seen but "all the brightness of the sun and moon," by which must be meant the mystery of their conjunction. It may also be a veiled allusion to Apocalypse [Revelation] 21:23-24: "And the city had no need of the sun, neither of the moon, to shine in it: for the glory of God did lighten it, and the Lamb is the light thereof." . . . In the Apocalypse, therefore, the place of the sun and moon is taken by a supernatural light, the Lamb of God. Obviously some such supernatural light is meant in *Aurora*. But whereas in the Apocalypse it *takes the place* of the sun and moon, here it is *begotten* by the sun and moon, in accord with the classical alchemical formula.[184]

Depicted in the unconscious imagery of the *Aurora*, in von Franz's view, is a psychological portrait of the swing of history from the first epoch to the second.[185] As mentioned, the darkness at the beginning of the visions anticipates that a spiritualized Christianity would become increasingly meaningless to more and more people over the next thousand-year period of Western history. Thus von Franz's supposition is that these images in the unconscious of Aquinas are truly prophetic, evocative of the fate of the Church that he loved so much. The vision picks up the pendulum beginning to sway away from the vertical, spiritual Christian viewpoint toward a rebirth of materialism. But this

---

[183] Is it any wonder that the heroine and succssor to Christ in the wildly popular novel *The Da Vinci Code* is named Sophie?

[184] *Aurora Consurgens*, pp. 319f.

[185] Ibid., pt. II, chap. x.

materialism is itself preparation for another phase which is the synthesis of the spiritual and material. I will attempt to explain.

Images of light in dreams can represent understanding (as in "I see"), so the light in the vision would represent the "light" by which, or manner in which, life is understood. There are three different images of light implied in the sun and moon representation in the above vision. First, there is the light of the sun and the light of the moon, taking the sun and the moon separately and the light from them being a mixture of the two. Second, there is the light of the Lamb which in Apocalypse is said to replace the light of the sun and moon. Third, there is the light of the sun and moon, taken as the light from the union of the sun and the moon, a single light begotten from their union. Von Franz follows this angle in the third case because the *Aurora* text in general is filled with alchemical allusions. The narrator who had the visions was intimately familiar with alchemical symbolism, as quite likely was the historical Aquinas.[186] Thus because the vision is replete with alchemical imagery, von Franz interprets the third light, that of the sun and the moon in the vision, to refer, as it would in an alchemical text, to the product of the union of the sun and the moon, an indicator of the goal of alchemical transformation.[187]

Recall that these three kinds of light are interpreted as metaphors for the main orienting perspectives that have appeared successively in our civilization.

The first light, which is a mixture of the sun and the moon, represents the pagan attitude, the sun and the moon standing for the natural desires so commonly raised to the level of divinity in antiquity. The light stands for the general attitude of the period, but if we were to visualize what that attitude looked like in an individual, how would it appear in behavior? In the earlier example of the woman's affair and professional crisis, the "pagan" attitude

---

[186] Ibid., pp. 412ff.

[187] And also an indicator of the end process of psychological transformation as this material is understood symbolically in dream interpretation.

would have been just to enjoy the sensuality of the experience without reflecting upon its meaning.

The second light, which had no need of the sun and moon and shone independently, personifies the Christian point of view, which separated itself from the ancient worship of nature. Again to provide an analogy from the same woman, the second light would have been to repress her desire and avoid the experience of lust altogether.

The Renaissance, science and the age of discovery are again a return of the light from the sun and moon as the natural world elicited attention once again. Yet the real point of the return of the sun and moon is not simply as natural powers in and for themselves but as constituents preparing for a new union. Nature and desire returned, not to shed a natural light as in antiquity, but to enter into a synthesis, the product of which is yet a third light, a new way of understanding. The third kind of light is thus representative of the sort of awareness which is now our historical challenge to develop. This understanding is neither of pure nature (the sun and moon), nor of the spirit (the Lamb); it is a spirit encountered through natural desires, but not identical with them (from the union of the sun and moon). We saw this more complete experience, again to refer to the woman's case, in her both going through the affair and looking at the images it generated within her. These images led her to a new life which she could not have attained without that experience.[188]

In the *Aurora,* according to von Franz, the visions of "Thomas" symbolize not just his personal predicament, his being challenged away from a pietistic spirituality, something he could never have achieved in the Middle Ages anyway. Although that personal interpretation might be true in principle, she sees the deeper meaning as indicators of larger, historical trends. What we observe in the visions is an image of how our recognition and experience of

---

[188] The question often arises, "Does an erotic relationship have to be concretely lived out?" The answer to this always depends on individual circumstances, and beyond our present scope.

what is sacred should evolve. First there was the light of antiquity, then there was the Christian light; then the sun and the moon returned, not merely as entities unto themselves but as elements in the creation of a new light, a new kind of understanding; this is what is being prepared for us now, and this is what appeared in the vision. A light—a point of view—is to be born out of our wrestling with the forces of nature. Note that nature is not exactly the guide, that is, the light, but rather a guiding light is to be created out of a fascination with the forces of nature. The spirit has to be plucked out of matter, out of our instinctual relationship to the material events of life. The pendulum has swung from matter to the Christian spirit, now back to matter again for the purpose of directing us to the material world in order for us finally to find the spirit there. Thomas's vision shows us, as Western history would soon be moving from a spiritual to a material phase, that the upcoming material phase (our current period) was itself to be a transition to yet another step, to the foundation of matter as a new source of light.

A consideration of the *Aurora* text leads us to the same conclusion that we saw concerning Jung's analysis of the phases of Western history, namely the nature of the psychological task presented to us in the current historical moment.

**Kepler and Fludd**

Pauli was very interested in the processes of history that led to the birth of science, and in his writing he considers the historical shifts in the West. In his view, something fundamental was lost when early and medieval Christianity gave way to the empiricism and worldliness of science; and materialism replaced spirituality. To understand what had been lost he turned to a polemic between a scientist, Johannes Kepler, and an alchemist, Robert Fludd.

Kepler, a German, worked largely in Austria at the very beginning of the Scientific Revolution, when our grasp of the working of the solar system was being developed. The Pole Copernicus had already said that the sun rather than the earth was at the center of our solar system. The sun does not revolve around the earth; the planets revolve around the sun. He made this statement unofficially at the beginning of the sixteenth century and reissued it officially many years later.[189] Kepler continued that idea. What he worked out mathematically from astronomical data, and published in 1609 and 1619, was that the planets circle the sun in ellipses, not in circles.[190] In 1633, Galileo, for his support of the findings of Copernicus and Kepler, was condemned by the Inquisition to house arrest for the remainder of his life. The Church eventually reversed its position in 1983.[191]

Robert Fludd was an English alchemist living at the same time as Kepler. Whereas Kepler devoted his life to finding the regularity of the laws that governed the universe, Fludd hotly criticized him for these views because, in Fludd's opinion, there was a soul substance permeating everything, which Kepler ignored. In Fludd's image of the cosmos (figure 28), there were two fundamental principles of the universe, form and matter. Form, as the light principle, came from above, and matter, as the dark principle, dwelled on earth. Pauli, explaining Fludd's viewpoint, writes:

> Just as God is symbolically represented by an equilateral triangle so there is a second, reflected triangle below that represents the world.
>
> A constant struggle goes on between these polar opposites: from below, the material pyramid grows upward from the earth like a tree . . . . , at the same time the formal pyramid grows downward with its apex on the earth . . . . In the middle, the sphere of the sun, where these opposing principles just counterbalance each other, there is engendered . . . the mystery . . . of the *infans solaris* {the infant sun] which is at the same time the liberated world-soul. . . .
>
> Whatever is produced without knowledge of these mysteries is an arbitrary, subjective fiction.[192]

---

[189] J.J. O'Connor and E.F. Robertson, "Nicholaus Copernicus."

[190] J.V. Field, "Johannes Kepler."

[191] Jose Wudka, "Galileo and the Inquisition."

[192] "The Influence of Archetypal Ideas on the Scientific Theories of Kepler," in Pauli, *Writings on Physics and Philosophy*, pp. 244ff.

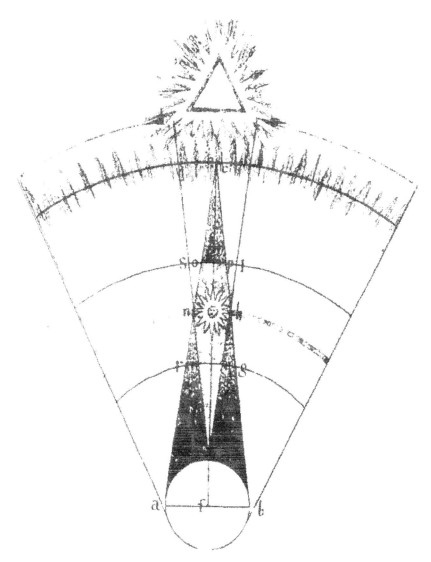

Figure 28. Robert Fludd's diagram of the cosmos.

Kepler's scientific viewpoint was a quantitative one; Fludd's prescientific viewpoint was a qualitative one. Fludd wrote: "I contemplate the internal and essential impulses that issue from nature herself."[193]

By examining the dispute between these two thinkers, Pauli observed the psychological aspect of the shift from the magical and religious thinking of the Middle Ages to the rational, scientific thinking which occurred in the fifteenth and sixteenth centuries. Prior to the scientific mind, the universe was thought to be permeated with a creative substance, a world soul, and it was this world soul that was thought to be the instigator of the physical movements of the planets and the earth. By the time the scientific method had taken precedence in the West, this world soul with its mystery and creative power had been excluded from our picture of space and time. Fludd held that there was no room for the mystery of events if everything was predictable as the outcome of immutable scientific laws. It is true that Kepler said that the regularity of the laws of the physical world was analogous to the lawfulness of God and was built on the pattern of God; still, this pattern was fixed; its constancy determined the regularity of earthly laws. For a medieval mind such as Fludd's, mathematical laws diminished the creativity and unpredictability of the world soul.

Pauli too held that science excluded an entire aspect of human experience from its field of inquiry. If mathematically-derived laws explain physical events on earth, where does that leave synchronicity, for example? How can there be such an experience as an unexpected and uncaused event in a world ruled by regular and causally explained laws? Pauli believed that the discovery of the unpredictability of electron movements in the atom was a step toward showing that there is a limit to the lawfulness of the universe.

In whatever way science will continue to develop in the future, and in whatever way our general view of life is to evolve as well,

---

[193] Ibid., p. 251.

Pauli felt that one of the main features of this development would be a recovery, in a way consistent with scientific methodology, of those aspects of human experience which defy causality and were lost during the Scientific Revolution.

We have seen that the excluded Stranger (Mercurius) and Sophia are still very much alive in the unconscious of Westerners. Pauli's experience is one example of "old" contents of the Western unconscious pressing for new life. They are our work, now. The world that was lost awaits rediscovery and expression in a new idiom as it challenges us to spiral forward into a fresh understanding.

Investigating a moment in history when epochs were colliding, Pauli, like Jung, was keenly aware of the effect of historical factors on psychological growth. He sought to learn from a previous transition of eons how our current one might be conceptualized and best addressed. He wanted to learn what the birth of the spirit out of matter would mean for the development of science and for his own life—achieving more success with the former than the latter. Pauli saw in the Kepler-Fludd polemic intimations of a lost part of life that awaited rediscovery, a lost spirit to repopulate the matter that science investigates. In *Aurora Consurgens*, too, we can see the birth of the spirit out of material principles. Both Pauli's dreams and the *Aurora* visions anticipate the psychological task of our time: the return of a spirit, brought back by our relation to matter.

In Pauli's dreams we see reflections of his creativity. Creative individuals are often the first to manifest a major cultural shift.[194] By evaluating what at first appear to be personal conflicts, creative individuals glimpse in their own personality an example of their society as a whole; they recognize that problems and forces within themselves parallel historic changes. In beginning to solve these challenges in an individual way, the creative person inwardly generates a small example of the kind of change that the society at

---

[194] Jung's visions at the beginning of World War One are exemplary. See *Memories, Dreams, Reflections*, chap. 6, "Confrontation with the Unconscious."

large will face. It is the existence of this "shift to the *for intérieur*" [French, "one's heart of hearts"][195] on the part of creative personalities that the British historian Arnold Toynbee has identified as the mark of a healthy society. What he writes in his massive study of the rise and fall of civilizations (conceived in 1919,[196] a meaningful time) is worth quoting at length:

> The presentation of each problem is a challenge to undergo an ordeal . . . . True growth consists in a progressive change of emphasis and transfer of energy and shifting of the scene of action out of the field of the macrocosm and into that of the microcosm; and in this new arena victorious responses to challenges do not take the form of overcoming an external obstacle, but manifest themselves in a progressive self-articulation. . . . The social catastrophe of disintegration thus reveals itself finally as a crisis of perception in the individual soul. . . . When the *élan* of growth in a healthy society seems to have given out, the passive individual loses his bearings . . . . but the alternative reaction is . . . to look inwards to the soul's own self . . . . It is not, then, by seeking to escape suffering, but by embracing and responding to it, that the soul born into a disintegrating society can win release and regain, on a higher plane, the path of growth from which the society has strayed.[197]

This could not be more clearly seen than in the life and work of Wolfgang Pauli. His personal struggle to find the spirit involved the fire he felt for Marie-Louise von Franz and its meaning of showing him the way toward a new professorship. He knew that the basic supposition of quantum mechanics opened the possibility of spirit in matter. His physics recognized that there are no laws that govern all motion, though science as yet has not found a way to conceptualize meaningful chance events. The challenge to Pauli's psychological life is thus a mirror image of the challenge science faces in its future evolution. His personal and professional struggles

---

[195] Arnold Toynbee, *A Study of History: The One-Volume Edition, Illustrated*, p. 140.

[196] William H. McNeill, *Arnold J. Toynbee: A Life*, p. 90.

[197] *A Study of History*, pp. 41, 137, 249, 254.

reflect and anticipate what our science—and society—are increasingly called to address. His conflicts, in large measure, are our conflicts. By studying his attempts to integrate forgotten truths, we learn about ourselves and our time.

## Jung's spiritual testament

As Pauli wrote: "More and more I see the psycho-physical problem as the key to the overall spiritual situation of our age."[198]

Indeed, the psycho-physical problem has been the subject of our discussion all along. Alerted to its importance in a dream, I have attempted to address its presence and to synthesize its diverse manifestations from Jung's and Pauli's work through von Franz's interest in picking up and carrying on what they started. Remember, too, that Pauli's introduction to these questions began when he fell into despair after World War Two and asked his unconscious for help in discerning what had gone wrong, what had happened that his honored science could have ended up producing mushroom clouds over Japanese cities.

In looking at the answers provided by the unconscious, and at the background necessary for some kind of understanding of those answers, we have traversed Jung's concept of the archetype, of numbers, of the limits of the Church's Trinitarian theology; we have examined images of the Stranger/Mercurius, Zarathustra, dual mandalas and Sophia. We have looked at all those places where spirit and matter, subject and object, guidance and world were considered one; these can be the origins of a new outlook on life.

Matter is now asking us to make the material world, the events of physical life, our locus for discerning the guidance of the spirit. Unlike Nietzsche, who fell into despair at the death of God announced by Zarathustra, and unlike Pauli who rather collapsed under the loneliness of the enterprise, Jung kept searching through the dark nights of the twentieth century until he found the new place of divinity's expression.

---

[198] *Atom and Archetype*, p. 81.

It is not true that we are cut off from meaning and purpose in what appears to be a secular age. There is an intelligence beside our waking and rational capacities which still speaks, but this intelligence has changed its point of entry into our lives. For more and more people, the spirit no longer comes down from above. It emerges up from matter and is there for those who are willing to accept the earth's complications and see the spirit in the storms body and matter throw at us. This is Jung's contribution to us and our time. Matter is now the vehicle of deeper knowledge, and for that we must stoop to muddy our hands in life's colorful clay. Then the guiding spirit speaks. But at last the old paradigm of subject versus object is finished.

In Jung's work are seeds for the beginning of yet another period of history, one in which humanity—and the earth itself—might have a chance to survive. When, as subjects, we realize that we too can be objects, and when we know how that feels, we change. When we know matter as a subject, not just as an object, we are no longer the same.

Suitably, it was a once-cynical physicist, the suffering nuclear scientist Wolfgang Pauli, who called the investigation of meaning in matter Jung's "spiritual testament."[199]

---

[199] Pauli's letter to Markus Fierz, in L.V. Laurikainen, *Beyond the Atom: The Philosophical Thought of Wolfgang Pauli,* pp. 142, 225.

# Postscript
## Future Challenges

Jung wrote in his autobiography: "The question of the chthonic spirit has occupied me ever since I began to delve into the world of alchemy."[200] We earlier met the chthonic spirit in Pauli's description of Mercurius and the Stranger, figures representing the symbolic dimension of matter. This unity of spirit and matter has been addressed in a number of writings in Jungian psychology, and the following are primary sources for additional exploration.

*Atom and Archetype: The Pauli/Jung Letters, 1932-1958*, the collected letters of Jung and Pauli edited by Jung's close associate and Pauli's friend, C.A. Meier, is the most important document for further inquiry. The book is not easy reading, but it is well worth the effort.

Jung's reflections on the psychoid archetype are contained in "On the Nature of the Psyche" (1954) in volume 8 of his *Collected Works*, entitled *The Structure and Dynamics of the Psyche*. His two essays on synchronicity in the same volume are also very instructive, with the shorter one, "On Synchronicity" (1952), being the most accessible.

A collection of Pauli's papers has been published under the title *Writings on Physics and Philosophy*. Three essays in that book are particularly readable: "Science and Western Thought" (1955), "Ideas of the Unconscious from the Standpoint of Natural Science and Epistemology" (1954), and "The Influence of Archetypal Ideas on the Scientific Theories of Kepler" (1952).

Marie-Louise von Franz's works are seminal and intriguing: *On Divination and Synchronicity* (1969 lectures published in 1980), *Number and Time* (1974), and *Projection and Recollection in*

---

[200] *Memories, Dreams, Reflections*, p. 168.

173

*Jungian Psychology* (1978). Collected papers dealing with her ideas on sprit and matter have been published as *Psyche and Matter* (1992). None of those works are difficult to follow, with the exception of *Number and Time*. That volume requires very careful and patient reading but, in the end, rewards the effort with a gold mine for further reflection.

David Lindorff, engineer and Jungian analyst, presents an enthusiastic and deep understanding of ground-breaking discoveries about the nature of the psyche and its relationship with the material world in *Pauli and Jung: The Meeting of Two Great Minds* (2004).

As for the future, undoubtedly research into the symbolism of the Stranger will yield a rich harvest. The examination of dreams involving Mercurius or figures similar to Pauli's Stranger will continue to show the unity of matter and spirit from new perspectives. Likewise, the other images I have considered—the lower trinity, number symbolism, dual mandalas, Sophia, etc.—all ask for further comparative research both mythologically and from analytic practice in terms of dreams. The occurrence of synchronicity in the analytic process and the dreams that accompany them is still a wide open field.

New dimensions and connections within spirit and matter are slowly manifesting themselves to the discerning eye, giving us a larger picture of life in general and of the analytic process in particular. Faced with the enormity of reevaluating the West's fundamental assumptions, and in light of the time that this might take, we can easily slip into nonchalance or simply feel overwhelmed. "What can *I* do?" we ask. When I feel that way, I recall a letter written to his wife by the playwright Václav Havel, the man who eventually became first president of the free Czech republic, as he sat in prison for crimes against the Communist state (that is, speaking the truth):

> If I consider the problem as that which the world is turning me into—that is, as a tiny screw in a giant machine, deprived of human identity—then there is really nothing I can do. Obviously I cannot

put a stop to the destruction of the globe, the growing stupidity of nations and the production of thousands of new thermonuclear bombs. If, however, I consider it as that which each of us originally is, or rather what each of us—irrespective of the state of the world—has the basic potential to become, which is to say an autonomous human being, capable of acting responsibly to and for the world, then of course there is a great deal I can do.[201]

We close, then, where we begin and end the journey, with "that which each of us originally is," and with the spirit at the heart of matter calling to the "great deal I can do."

Figure 29. Mercurius in the alchemical retort.

---

[201] Havel, *Letters to Olga*, p. 295.

# Acknowledgments

I would like to thank Cynthia Swartz, Linda Milburn and Victoria Cowan for their invaluable help with the evolving manuscript. Sincere appreciation is also due Daryl Sharp, Marion Woodman, David Lindorff and Edward F. Edinger; their consistently creative work has never failed to inspire. Finally, without the commitment of my analysands and Indianapolis seminars this book could not have been written.

# Bibliography

*All Things Considered*. National Public Radio. May 6, 2003. Radio broadcast.

Magnus, Bernd. "Friedrich Nietzsche." In *Encyclopædia Britannica 2003 Deluxe Edition CD-ROM*. New York: Encyclopædia Britannica, Inc., 1994-2002.

*The Diane Rehm Show*. National Public Radio. March 26, 2003. Radio broadcast.

Edinger, Edward F. *Ego and Archetype*. New York: Penguin Books, 1973.

_____. *The Psyche in Antiquity, Book 2: Gnosticism and Early Christianity*. Toronto: Inner City Books, 1999.

_____. *Transformation of the God Image*. Toronto: Inner City Books, 1992.

Edwards, Tony. *The Case of ESP*. WGBH Boston/BBC coproduction, 1984. Videorecording.

Eliot, T.S. "Four Quartets," *The Complete Poems and Plays, 1909-1950*. New York: Harcourt, Brace & World, 1971.

Enz, Charles P. Interview. In *The Psychlogy of Jung: Passions of the Soul, Mind and Matter*. Ikon television. Videorecording. Princeton:Films for the Humanities, 1992.

_____. *No Time To Be Brief: A Scientific Biography of Wolfgang Pauli*. Oxford: Oxford University Press, 2002.

_____. *Pauli hat gesagt: Eine Biographie des Nobelpreisträgers Wolfgang Pauli, 1900-1958*. Zürich: Verlag Neue Züricher Zeitung, 2005.

Field, J.V. "Johannes Kepler." [http://www-history.mcs.st-and.ac.uk/~history/Biographies/Kepler.html]. August 2006.

Frayn, Michael. *Copenhagen*. KCET Hollywood/BBC coproduction, 2002. Videorecording: http://www.shoppbs.org/sm-pbs-copenhagen-vhs--pi-1403382.html.

Freud, Sigmund. *New Introductory Lectures on Psycho-Analysis*. Trans. James Strachey. New York: W.W. Norton, 1965.

Frey, L., and Schärf, R., eds., *The Psychological Interpretation of Children's Dreams: Notes on Lectures Given by Prof. Dr. C.G. Jung at the Eidgenosische Technische Hochschule.* Trans. M. Foote and C. Brunner. Zürich: privately printed, 1938-39.

Frey-Rohn, Liliane. *From Freud to Jung.* Trans. F.E. Engreen and E.K. Engreen. New York: C.G. Jung Foundation, 1974.

Havel, Václav. *Letters to Olga.* Trans. Paul Wilson. New York: Henry Holt, 1989.

Howell, Alice O. *The Heavens Declare: Astrological Ages and the Evolution of Consciousness.* Wheaton, IL: Quest Books, 2006.

Jaffé, Aniela. *C.G. Jung: Word and Image.*(Bollingend Series XCVII.2). Princeton: Princeton University Press, 1983.

Jung, C.G. *The Collected Works* (Bollingen Series XX). 20 vols. Trans. R.F.C. Hull. Ed. H. Read, M. Fordham, G. Adler, Wm. McGuire. Princeton: Princeton University Press, 1953-1979.

_____. *Letters* (Bollingen Series XCV). 2 vols. Trans. R.F.C. Hull. Ed. G. Adler, A. Jaffé. Princeton: Princeton University Press, 1973.

_____. *Memories, Dreams, Reflections.* Ed. Aniela Jaffé. New York: Vintage Books, 1965.

_____. *Nietzsche's* Zarathustra: *Notes of the Seminar Given in 1934-1939* (Bollingen Series XCIC). 2 vols. Ed. J.L. Jarrett. Princeton: Princeton University Press, 1988.

_____. *Psychology of the Unconscious: A Study of Transformations and Symbols of the Libido* (Bollingen Series XX). Supplementary volume B of *The Collected Works.* Trans. B. Hinkle. Ed. William McGuire. Princeton: Princeton University Press: 1991.

_____. *Visions: Notes of the Seminar Given in 1930-1934* (Bollingen Series XCIX). 2 vols. Ed. C. Douglas. Princeton: Princeton University Press, 1997.

Jung, C.G. and Wilhelm, Richard. *The Secret of the Golden Flower.* Trans. R. Wilhelm and C. Baynes. London: Routledge and Kegan Paul, 1962.

King, Ursula. *Spirit of Fire: The Life and Vision of Teilhard de Chardin.* Maryknoll, New York: Orbis Books, 1966.

Koller, John M. and Koller, Patricia Joyce. *Asian Philosophies.* Third ed. Upper Saddle River, NJ: Prentice Hall, 1998.

Laurikainen, L.V. *Beyond the Atom: The Philosophical Thought of Wolfgang Pauli.* Trans. E. Holman. New York: Springer Verlag, 1985.

Lindorff, David. *Pauli and Jung: The Meeting of Two Great Minds.* Wheaton, IL: Quest Books, 2004.

March, Robert H. *Physics for Poets.* 2$^{nd}$ ed. Chicago: Contemporary Books, 1978.

McNeill, William H. *Arnold J. Toynbee: A Life.* Oxford: Oxford University Press, 1989.

Meier, C.A., ed. *Atom and Archetype: The Pauli/Jung Letters 1932-1958.* Trans. D. Roscoe. Princeton: Princeton University Press, 2001

_____. *The Unconscious in Its Empirical Manifestations.* Trans. E. Rolfe. Boston: Sigo Press, 1984.

Nietzsche, Friedrich. *Thus Spake Zarathustra.* Trans. T. Common. New York: The Modern Library, n.d.

O'Connor, J.J. and Robertson, E.F. "Nicholaus Copernicus." On internet: [http://www.gap.dcs.stand.ac.uk/~history/Biographies/Copernicus.html]. August 2006.

Pais, Abraham. "Wolfgang Pauli." In *The Genius of Science.* Oxford: Oxford University Press, 2000.

Pauli, Wolfgang. *Writings on Physics and Philosophy.* Trans. R. Schlapp. Ed. C.P. Enz, K. von Meyenn. New York: Springer Verlag, 1994.

Reese, Ellen P. and Bateson, P.P.G. *Imprinting.* Appleton-Century-Crofts/Meredith Corporation, 1968. Videorecording.

Shalit, Erel. *The Complex: From Archetype to Ego.* Toronto: Inner City Books, 2002.

Sharp, Daryl. *Digesting Jung: Food for the Journey.* Toronto: Inner City Books, 2001.

_____. *Jungian Psychology Unplugged: My Life as an Elephant.* Toronto: Inner City Books, 1998.

Stevens, Anthony. *Archetype Revisited: An Updated Natural History of the Self.* Toronto: Inner City Books, 2003.

Sweeney, Brian and Owens, Jacqueline. "Ernest Rutherford: Atom Man," [http://www.nzedge.com/heroes/rutherford.html]. August 2006.

Toynbee, Arnold. *A Study of History: The One-Volume Edition,*

*Illustrated*. London: Thames and Hudson, 1988.

van der Post, Laurens and Pottiez, Jean-Marc. *A Walk with a White Bushman*. New York: William Morrow, 1986.

van der Post, Laurens and Taylor, Jane. *Testament to the Bushman*. Middlesex, U.K.: Penguin Books, 1985.

van Erkelens, Herbert. "The Spirit of Matter." In *Psychological Perspectives*, no. 24 (Spring Summer 1991).

_____. "Wolfgang Pauli and the Chinese *Anima* Figure." *Eranos Yearbook 1999*. Ed. J.G. Donat, J.F. Livernois. Woodstock, CT: Spring Audio and Journal, 1999.

_____. "Wolfgang Pauli, the Feminine and the Perils of the Modern Soul." *Harvest: Journal for Jungian Studies*. Vol. 48, no. 2 (2002).

_____. *Wolfgang Pauli und der Geist der Materie*. Würzburg: Königshausen und Neumann, 2002.

von Franz, Marie-Louise. *Alchemy: An Introduction to the Symbolism and the Psychology*. Toronto: Inner City Books, 1980.

_____, ed. *Aurora Consurgens*. Trans. R.F.C. Hull and A.S. B. Glovr. Toronto: Inner City Books, 2000.

_____. "Bollingen, September 1982." Videorecording. Zürich: Stiftung für Jung'sche Psychologie,. 1982.

_____. *Number and Time: Reflections Leading Towards a Unification of Psychology and Physics*. Trans. A. Dykes. Evanston, IL: Northwestern University Press, 1974.

_____. *On Divination and Synchronicity: The Psychology of Meaningful Chance*. Toronto: Inner City Books, 1980.

_____. *Projection and Recollection in Jungian Psychology: Reflections of the Soul*. Trans. W.H. Kennedy. La Salle, IL: Open Court, 1980.

_____. *Psyche and Matter*. Boston: Shambhala, 1992.

von Meyenn, Karl, ed., *Wolgang Pauli. Wissenschaftlicher Briefwechsel mit Bohr, Einstein, Heisenberg u.a.* Band IV/Teil I. Berlin: Springer Verlag, 1950-1952.

Wehr, *Jung: An Illustrated Biography*. Boston: Shambhala, 1989.

Wilhelm, Richard, trans. *The I Ching or Book of Changes*. Rendered into English by C.F. Baynes. London: Routledge and Kegan Paul, 1968.

Wilhelm, Richard and Wilhelm, Hellmut. *Understanding the I Ching* (Bollingen Series XIX:2). Princeton: Princeton University Press, 1988.

Wudka, Jose. "Galileo and the Inquisition." [http://physics.ucr.edu/~wudka/Physics7/Notes_www/node52.html]. August 2006.

Zypolitas, Emmanuel Kennedy, ed., *The Fountain of the Love of Wisdom: An Homage to Marie-Louise von Franz.* Wilmette, IL: Chiron Publicatons, 2006.

# Index

Entries in *italics* refer to illustrations

# Also in this Series, by Marie-Louise von Franz

# Also in this Series, by Edward F. Edinger

# Also in this Series, by James Hollis

**THE MIDDLE PASSAGE: From Misery to Meaning in Midlife**
ISBN 0-919123-60-0. (1993) 128pp. *Sewn* $22
Why do so many go through so much disruption in their middle years? Why then? What does it mean and how can we survive it? Hollis shows how we can pass through midlife consciously, rendering the second half of life all the richer and more meaningful.

**UNDER SATURN'S SHADOW: The Wounding and Healing of Men**
ISBN 0-919123-64-3. (1994) 144pp. *Sewn* $22
Saturn was the Roman god who ate his children to stop them from usurping his power. Men have been psychologically and spiritually wounded by this legacy. Hollis offers a new perspective on the secrets men carry in their hearts, and how they may be healed.

**TRACKING THE GODS: The Place of Myth in Modern Life**
ISBN 0-919123-69-4. (1995) 160pp. *Sewn* $22
Whatever our religious background or personal psychology, a greater intimacy with myth provides a vital link with meaning. Here Hollis explains why a connection with our mythic roots is crucial for us as individuals and as responsible citizens.

**SWAMPLANDS OF THE SOUL: New Life in Dismal Places**
ISBN 0-919123-74-0. (1996) 160pp. *Sewn* $22
Much of our time on earth we are lost in the quicksands of guilt, anxiety, betrayal, grief, doubt, loss, loneliness, despair, anger, obsessions, addictions, depression and the like. Perhaps the goal of life is not happiness but meaning. Hollis illuminates the way.

**THE EDEN PROJECT: In Search of the Magical Other**
ISBN 0-919123-80-5. (1998) 160pp. *Sewn* $22
A timely and thought-provoking corrective to the fantasies about relationships that permeate Western culture. Here is a challenge to greater personal responsibility—a call for individual growth as opposed to seeking rescue from others.

**CREATING A LIFE: Finding Your Individual Path**
ISBN 0-919123-93-7. (2001) 160pp. *Sewn* $22
With insight and compassion grounded in the humanist side of analytical psychology, Hollis elucidates the circuitous path of individuation, illustrating how we may come to understand our life choices and relationships by exploring our core complexes.

**ON THIS JOURNEY WE CALL OUR LIFE: Living the Questions**
ISBN 1-894574-04-4. (2003) 160pp. *Sewn* $22
This book seeks a working partnership with readers. Hollis shares his personal experience only so that we may more deeply understand our own. It is a partnership rich in poetry as well as prose, but most of all it reminds us of the treasures of uncertainty.

# Also in this Series, by Daryl Sharp

*Prices and Payment in $US (except in Canada, $Cdn)*

THE SECRET RAVEN
Conflict and Transformation in the Life of Franz Kafka
ISBN 978-0-919123-00-7. (1980) 128 pp. $20

PERSONALITY TYPES: Jung's Model of Typology
ISBN 978-0-919123-30-9. (1987) 128 pp. Diagrams $22

THE SURVIVAL PAPERS: Anatomy of a Midlife Crisis
ISBN 978-0-919123-34-2. (1988) 160 pp. $22

DEAR GLADYS: The Survival Papers, Book 2
ISBN 978-0-919123-36-6. (1989) 144 pp. $22

JUNG LEXICON: A Primer of Terms and Concepts
ISBN 978-0-919123-48-9. (1991) 160 pp. Diagrams $22

GETTING TO KNOW YOU: The Inside Out of Relationship
ISBN 978-0-919123-56-4. (1992) 128 pp. $20

*THE BRILLIG TRILOGY:*

   1. CHICKEN LITTLE: The Inside Story *(A Jungian romance)*
   ISBN 978-0-919123-62-5. (1993) 128 pp. $20

   2. WHO AM I, REALLY? Personality, Soul and Individuation
   ISBN 978-0-919123-68-7. (1995) 144 pp. $22

   3. LIVING JUNG: The Good and the Better
   ISBN 978-0-919123-73-1. (1996) 128 pp. $20

JUNGIAN PSYCHOLOGY UNPLUGGED: My Life as an Elephant
ISBN 978-0-919123-81-6. (1998) 160 pp. $22

CUMULATIVE INDEX of Inner City Books: The First 80 Titles, 1980-1998
ISBN 978-0-919123-82-3. (1999) 160 pp. 8-1/2" x 11" $30

DIGESTING JUNG: Food for the Journey
ISBN 978-0-919123-96-0. (2001) 128 pp. $20

*THE SLEEPNOT TRILOGY:*

   1. NOT THE BIG SLEEP: On having fun, seriously *(A Jungian romance)*
   ISBN 978-0-894574-13-6. (2005) 128 pp. $20

   2. ON STAYING AWAKE: Getting Older and Bolder *(Another Jungian romance)*
   ISBN 978-0-894574-16-7. (2006) 144 pp. $20

   3. EYES WIDE OPEN: Late Thoughts *(Another Jungian romance)*
   ISBN 978-0-894574-18-1.. (2007) 160 pp. $25

*Please see next page for discounts and postage/handling.*

# Studies in Jungian Psychology
# by Jungian Analysts

*Quality Paperbacks*

*Prices and payment in $US (except in Canada, $Cdn)*

**Alchemy: An Introduction to the Symbolism and the Psychology**
*Marie-Louise von Franz (Zurich)* ISBN 978-0-919123-04-5. 288 pp. $30

**Jung and Yoga: The Psyche-Body Connection**
*Judith Harris (London, Ontario)* ISBN 978-0-919123-95-3. 160 pp. $22

**The Gambler: Romancing Lady Luck**
*Billye B. Currie (Jackson, MS)* 978-1-894574-19-8. 128 pp. $25

**Conscious Femininity: Interviews with Marion Woodman**
*Introduction by Marion Woodman (Toronto)* ISBN 978-0-919123-59-5. 160 pp. $22

**The Sacred Psyche: A Psychological Approach to the Psalms**
*Edward F. Edinger (Los Angeles)* ISBN 978-1-894574-09-9. 160 pp. $22

**Eros and Pathos: Shades of Love and Suffering**
*Aldo Carotenuto (Rome)* ISBN 978- 0-919123-39-7. 144 pp. $22

**Descent to the Goddess: A Way of Initiation for Women**
*Sylvia Brinton Perera (New York)* ISBN 978-0-919123-05-2. 112 pp. $20

**Addiction to Perfection: The Still Unravished Bride**
*Marion Woodman (Toronto)* ISBNj 978-0-919123-11-3. Illustrated. 208 pp. $25/$30hc

**The Illness That We Are: A Jungian Critique of Christianity**
*John P. Dourley (Ottawa)* ISBN 978-0-919123-16-8. 128 pp. $20

**Coming To Age: The Croning Years and Late-Life Transformation**
*Jane R. Prétat (Providence)* ISBN 978-0-919123-63-2. 144 pp. $22

**Jungian Dream Interpretation: A Handbook of Theory and Practice**
*James A. Hall, M.D. (Dallas)* ISBN 978-0-919123-12-0. 128 pp. $22

**Phallos: Sacred Image of the Masculine**
*Eugene Monick (Scranton)* ISBN 978-0-919123-26-7. 30 illustrations. 144 pp. $22

**The Sacred Prostitute: Eternal Aspect of the Feminine**
*Nancy Qualls-Corbett (Birmingham)* ISBN 978-0-919123-31-1. Illustrated. 176 pp. $25

**Longing for Paradise: Psychological Perspectives on an Archetype**
*Mario Jacoby (Zurich)* ISBN 978-1-894574-17-4. 240 pp. $30

**The Pregnant Virgin: A Process of Psychological Development**
*Marion Woodman (Toronto)* ISBN 978-0-919123-20-5. Illustrated. 208 pp. $25pb/$30hc

*Discounts: any 3-5 books, 10%; 6-9 books, 20%; 10-19, 25%; 20 or more, 40%.*
*Add Postage/Handling: 1-2 books, $6 surface ($10 air); 3-4 books, $8 surface ($12 air); 5-9 books, $15 surface ($20 air); 10 or more, $10 surface ($25 air)*

Ask for free **Jung at Heart** newsletter and Catalogue describing **over 100 titles**

**INNER CITY BOOKS**
Box 1271, Station Q, Toronto, ON M4T 2P4, Canada

Tel. (416) 927-0355 / Fax (416) 924-1814 / E-mail: sales@innercitybooks.net